Sm;)e

DB Burkeman   *again...*   Rich Browd

**Some words from
Norman Cook (Fatboy Slim)**

I first began my obsession with the smiley in 1977 when I bought my first 12"
single, 'psycho killer' by the Talking Heads. It had a picture sleeve which was
simply a smiley t-shirt. I knew the image vaguely from growing up in the 60's
or 70's but this usage put it in a different cultural box now. It was not purely
a simplistic childish invocation to be regardlessly happy but a nod to the
history of it's usage. It summoned up the spirit of the hippie counterculture
of the 60's, the consumerist positivism of the 70's and, especially for a punk
band singing about a psycho killer, a new sense of IRONY.

Irony and history are (I believe) an enormous part of the smiley's cross-
cultural popularity. Whether the inane grin on a Banksy grim reaper or heavily
armed soldier or a cheap reference to the swinging 60's irony and history are
instantly summoned by two oval dots and a swish more than any icon in our
vocabulary. Everybody has an immediate subliminal response.

The smiley was created by Harvey Ball in 1963 as a symbol to the employees
of the State Mutual Life Assurance Company to keep morale up during a
takeover transition in the company. He was paid $45 for his work. 100 pin
badges were made and the icon was born. By 1971 an estimated 50 million
badges had been sold or given away featuring the design. Harvey Ball never
copyrighted or trademarked it because he believed it belonged to the people
and had a life all of its own. Though subsequently avaricious businessmen
have attempted to copyright it and charge people for its use it is impossible
to control because of its relationship with us all. It is part of our visual
language, it's an old friend who cheers us up and makes us grin...

The smiley is a symbol of (and forgive me for all the things I leave out
here.....) The 60's, the 70's, 90's acid house movement, The Watchmen,
Walmart, freedom, Nirvana, ecstacy pills, Marc Jacobs, the 'have a nice day'
movement, skaters, ravers, hippies, yippies, the (fictional) smiley killer (2012 film),
perseverance in the face of absurdity, Forrest Gump, the McGoven '72
campaign, the 'don't worry be happy' movement, Shoom club in London,
oh and Fat Boy Slim.

Long live the little fella and all who communicate with him, appropriate him,
wear him, paint him or just believe in him.
He belongs to all of us........

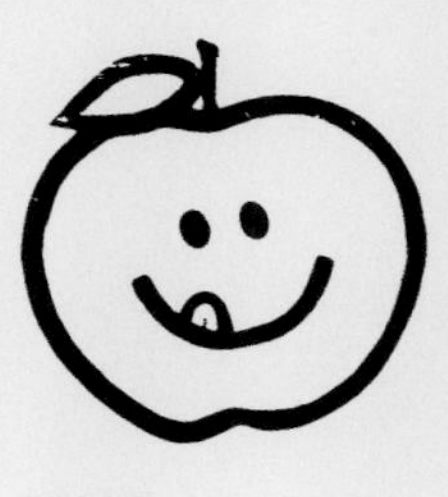
NO
PROBLEM!
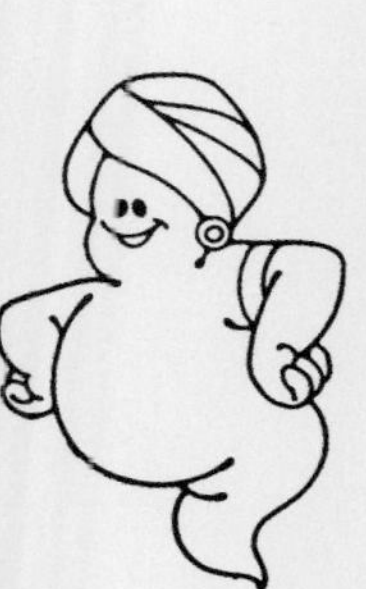
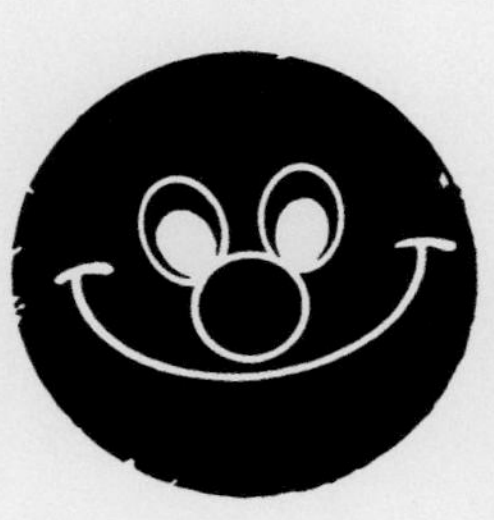
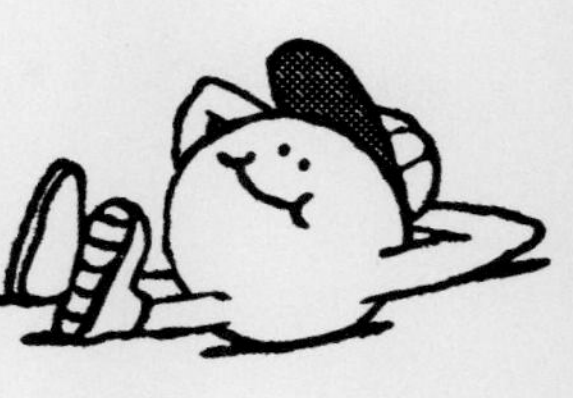

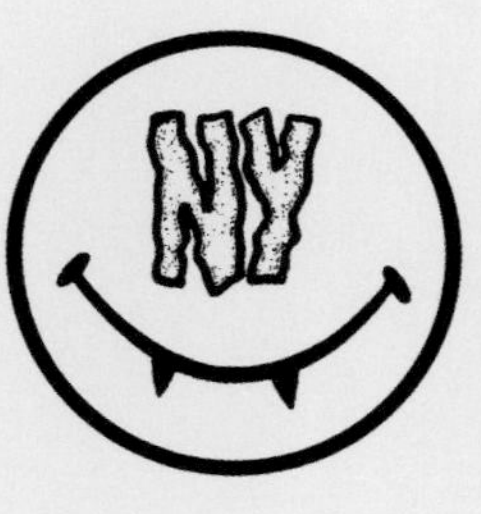
NY
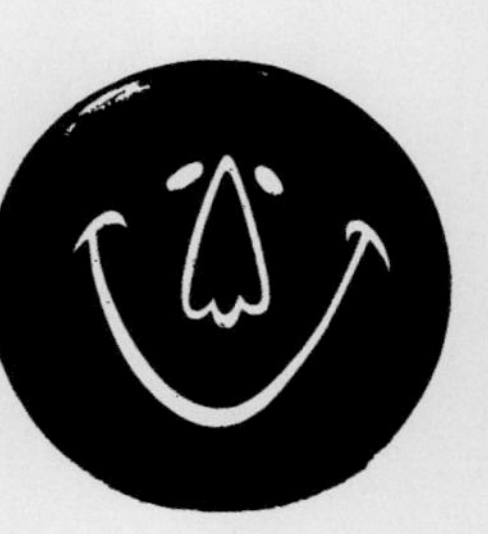
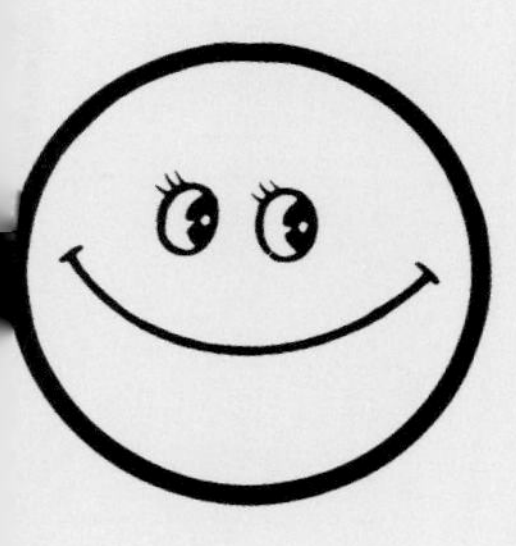

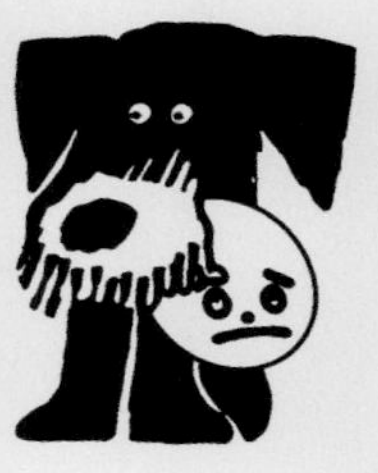
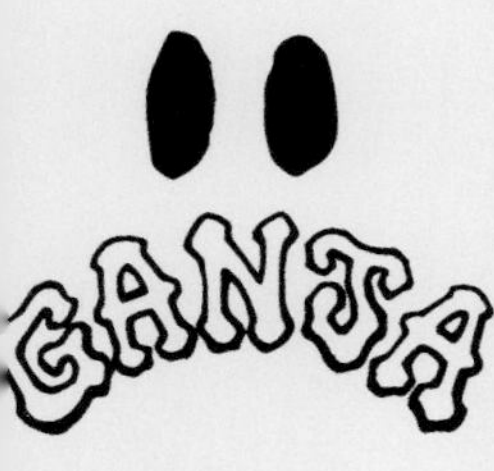
SANTA

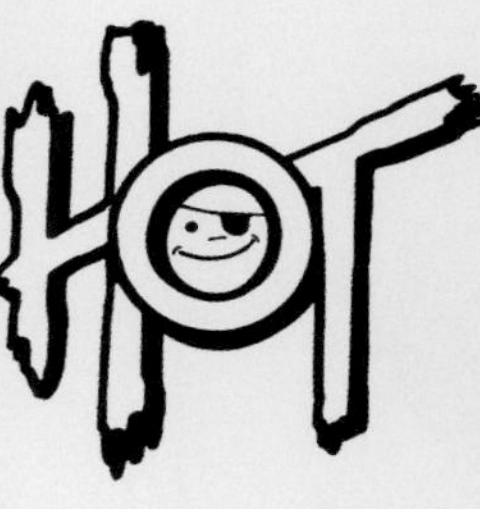
HOT

For our sons, Max Burkeman & Gus Browd, hope this makes you Sm;)e.

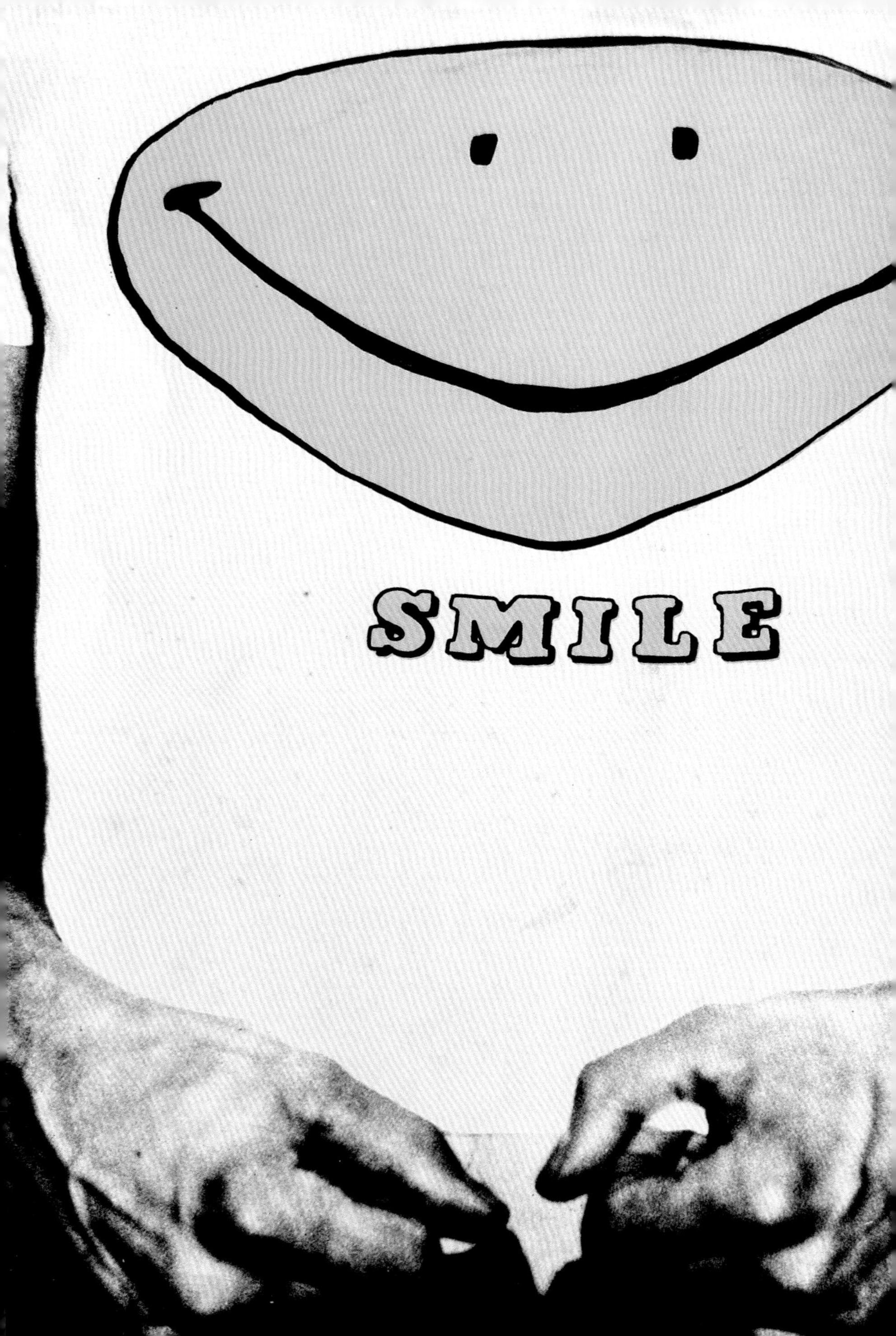

SMILE

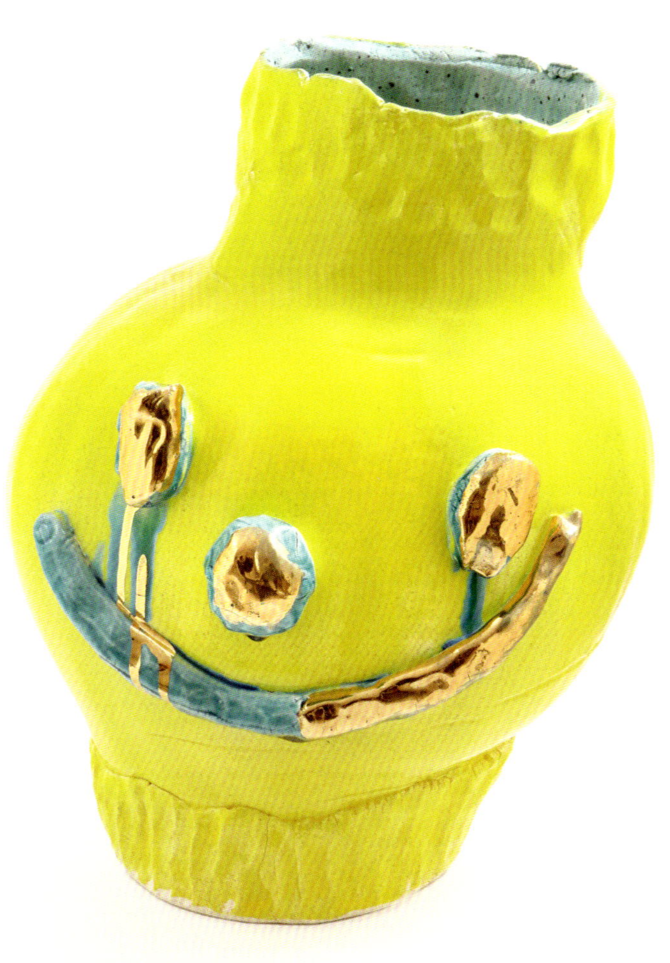

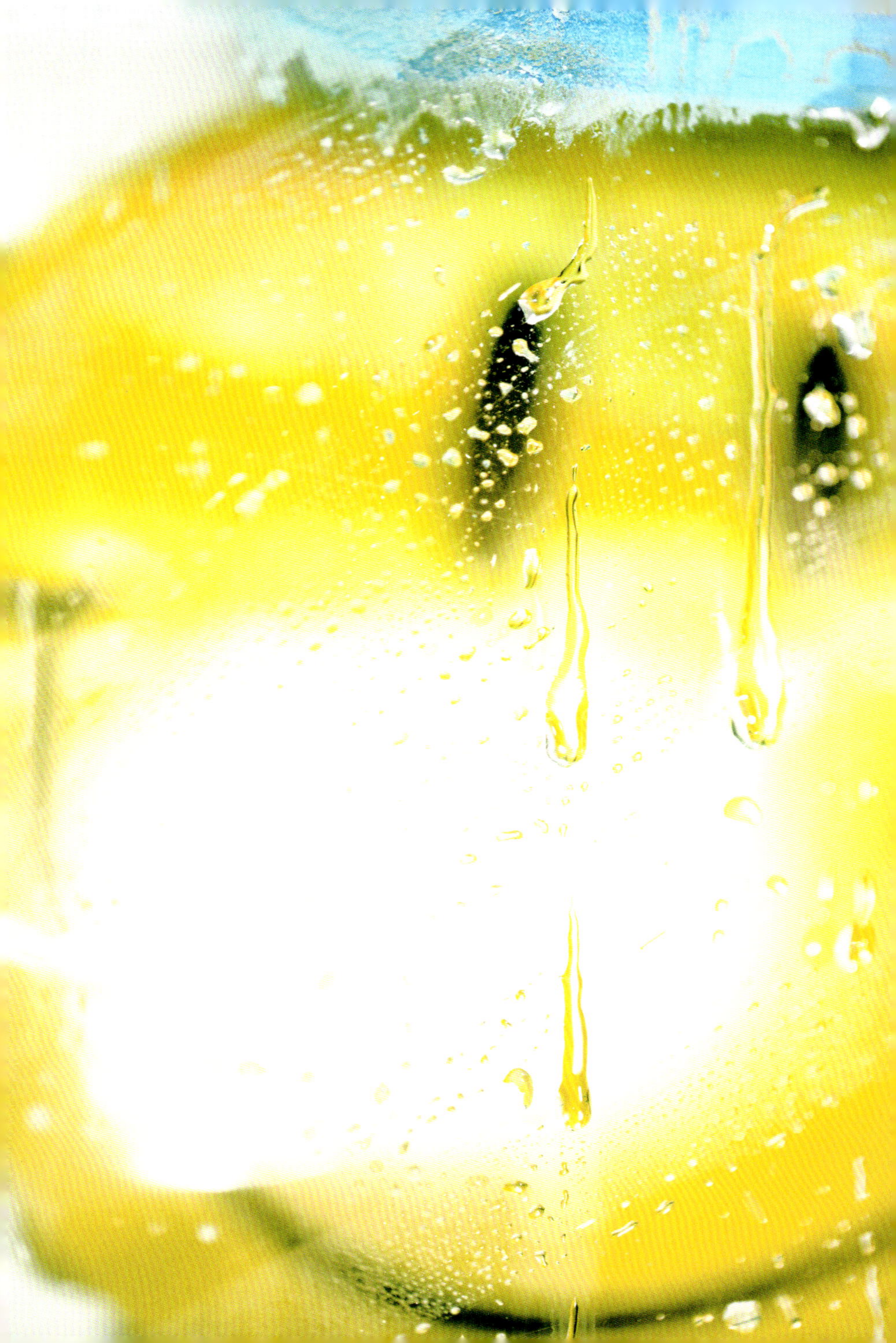

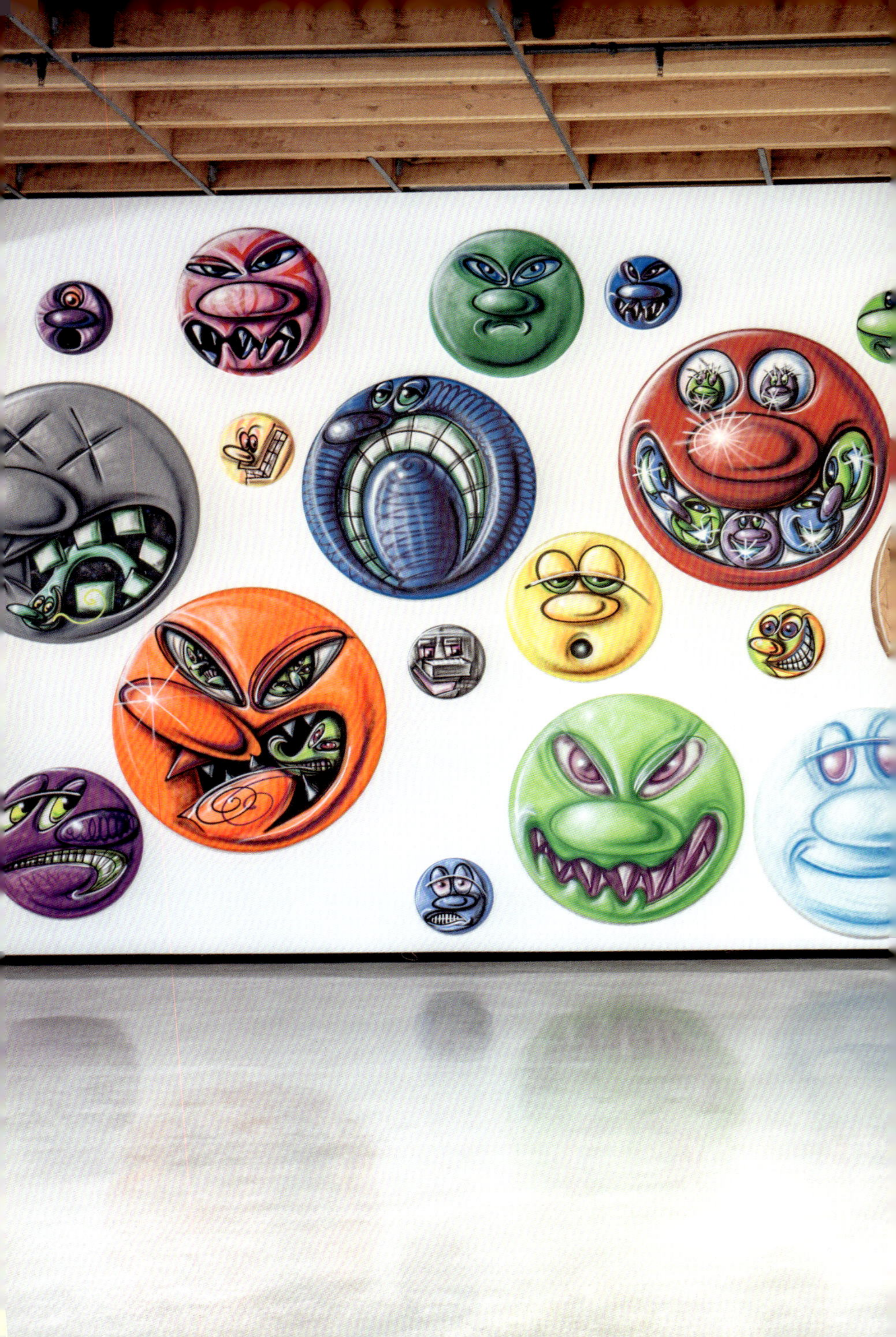

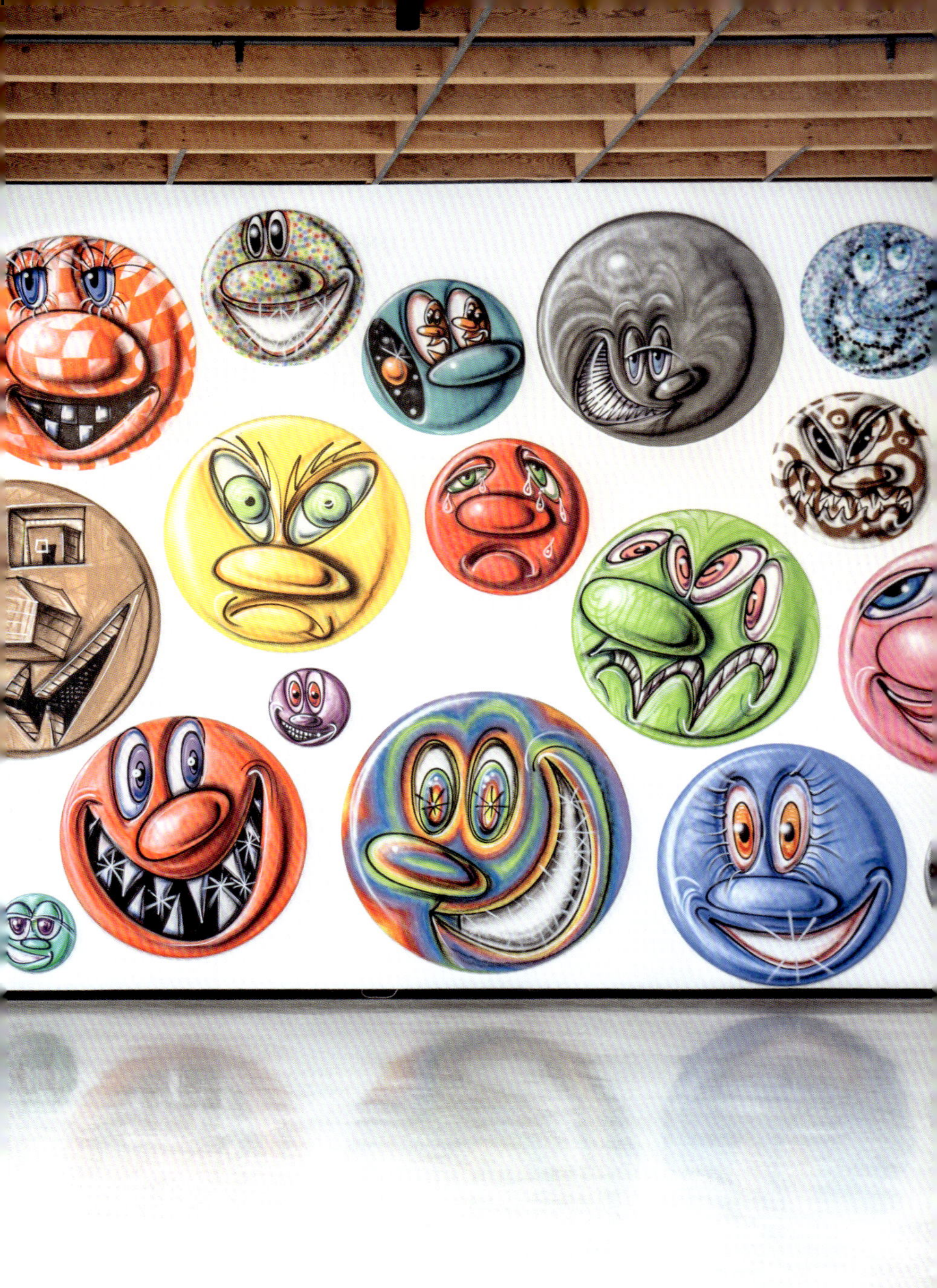

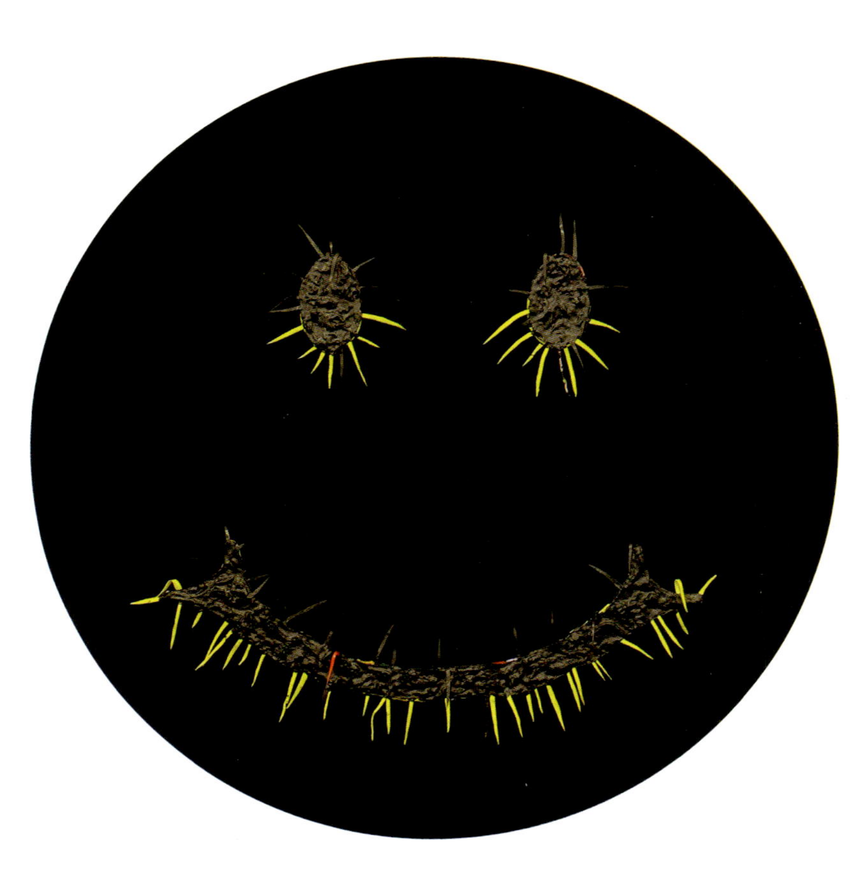

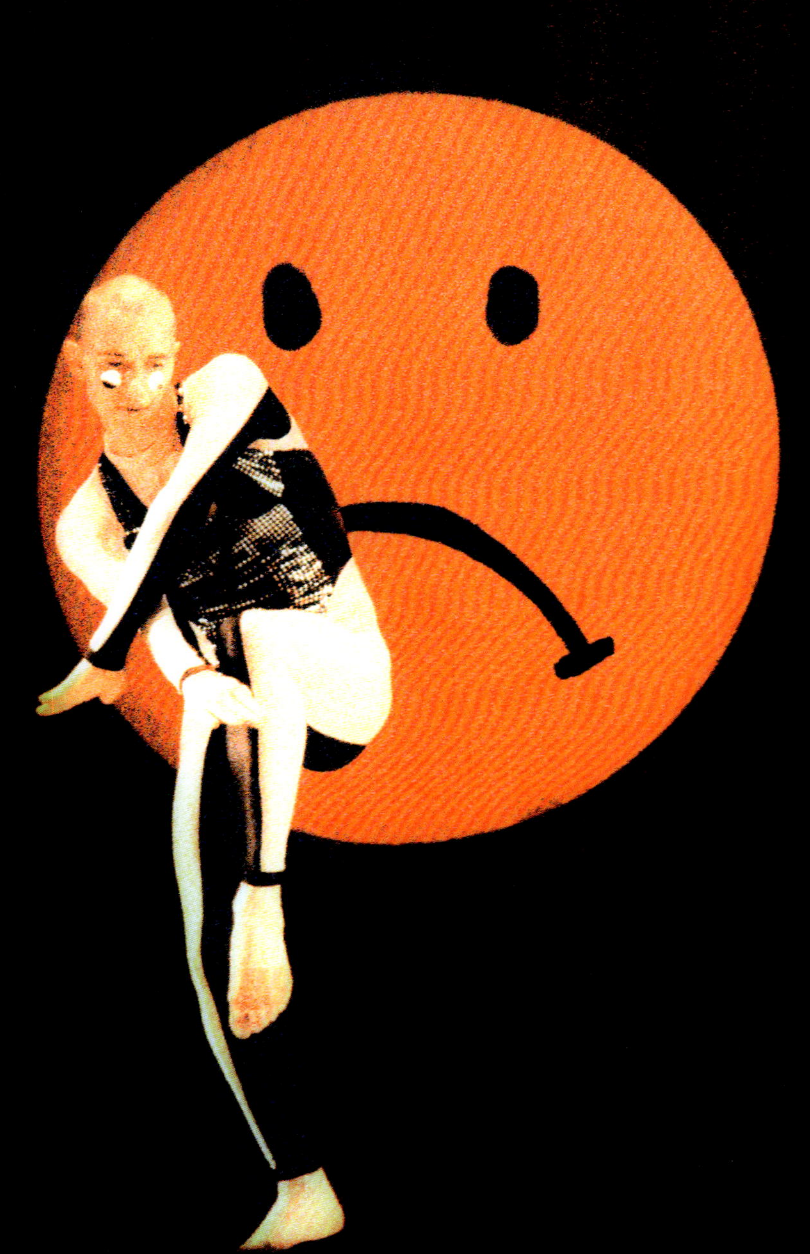

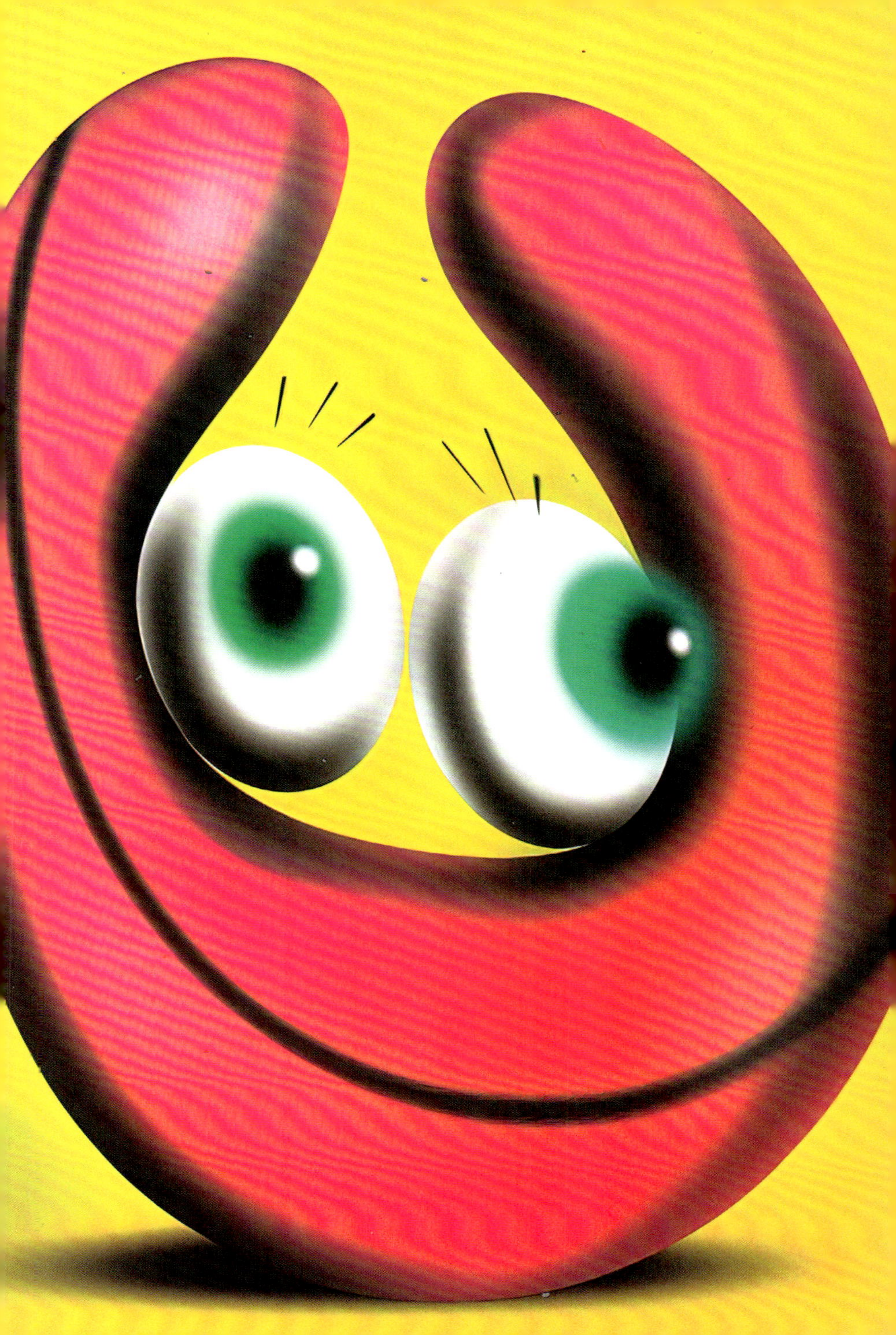

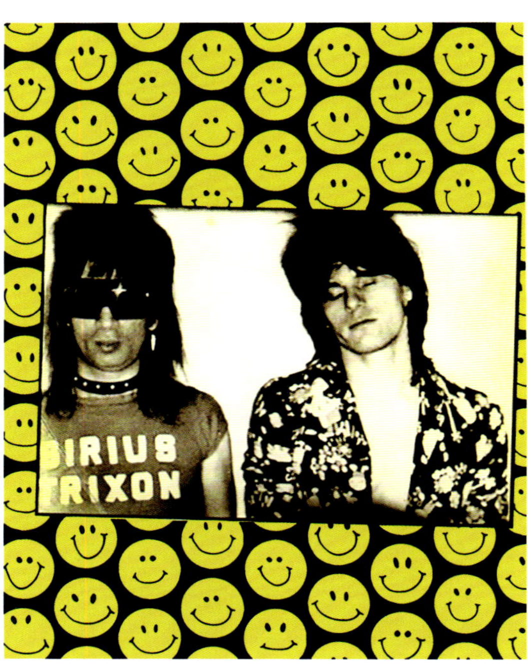
SIRIUS
TRIXON

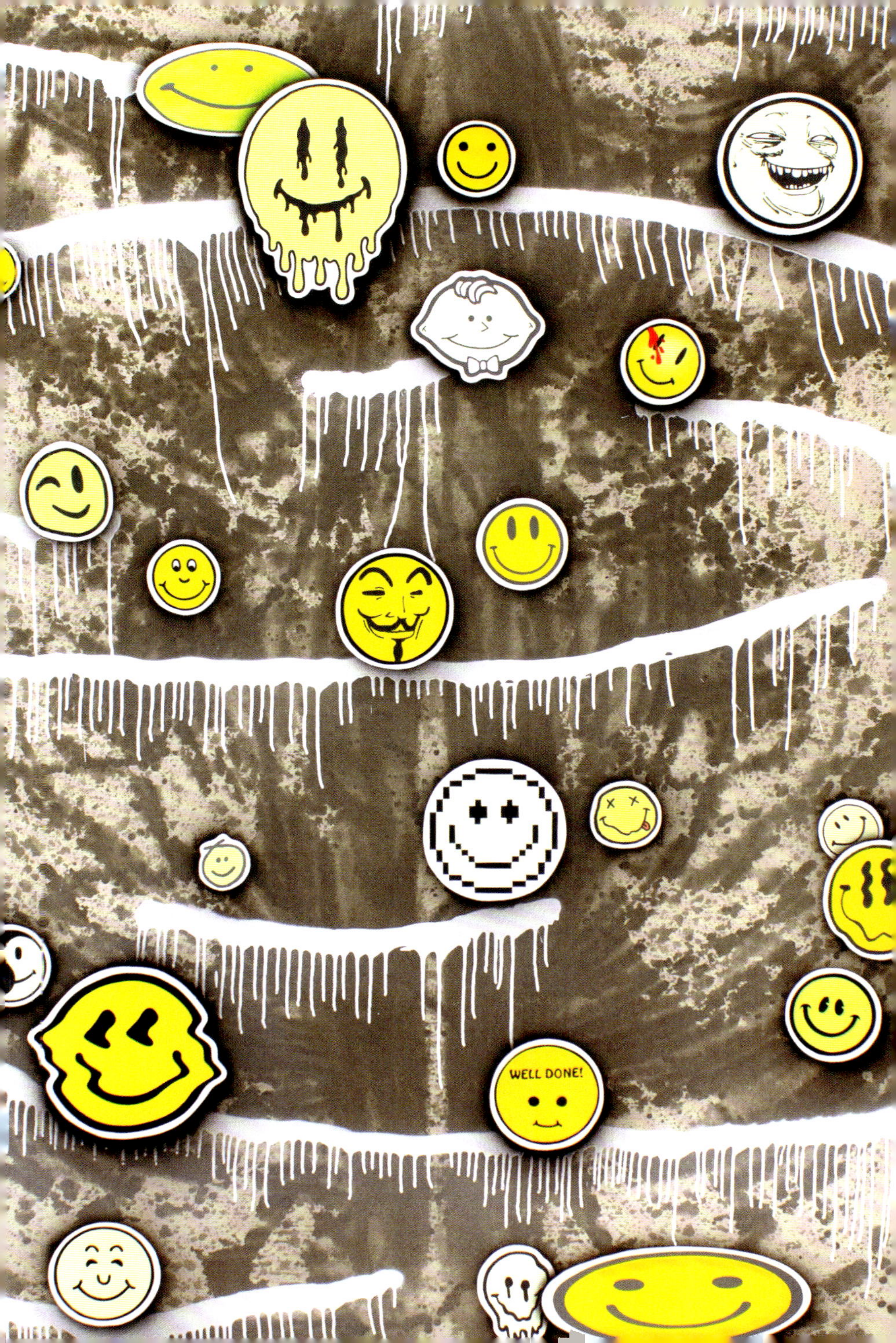
WELL DONE!

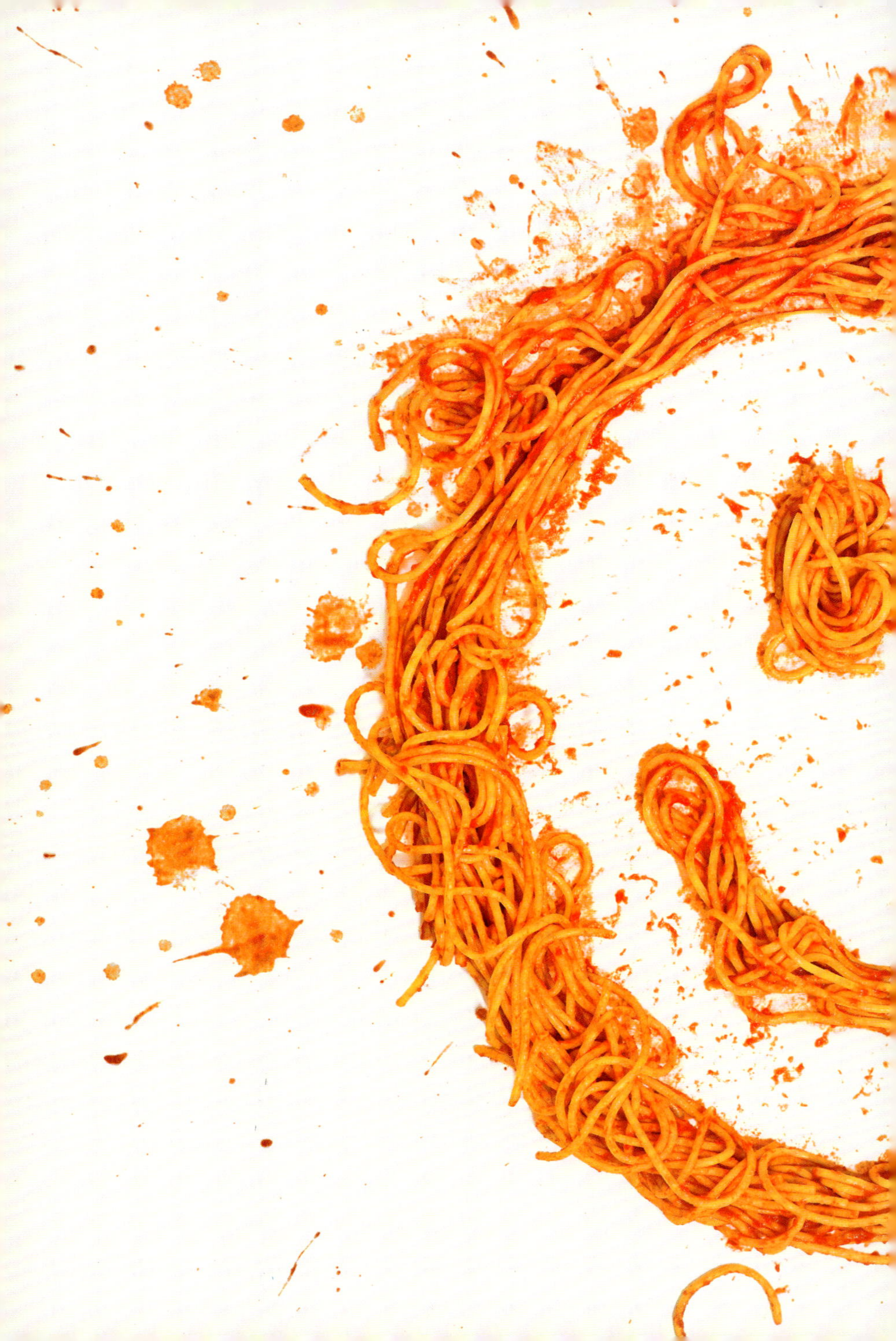

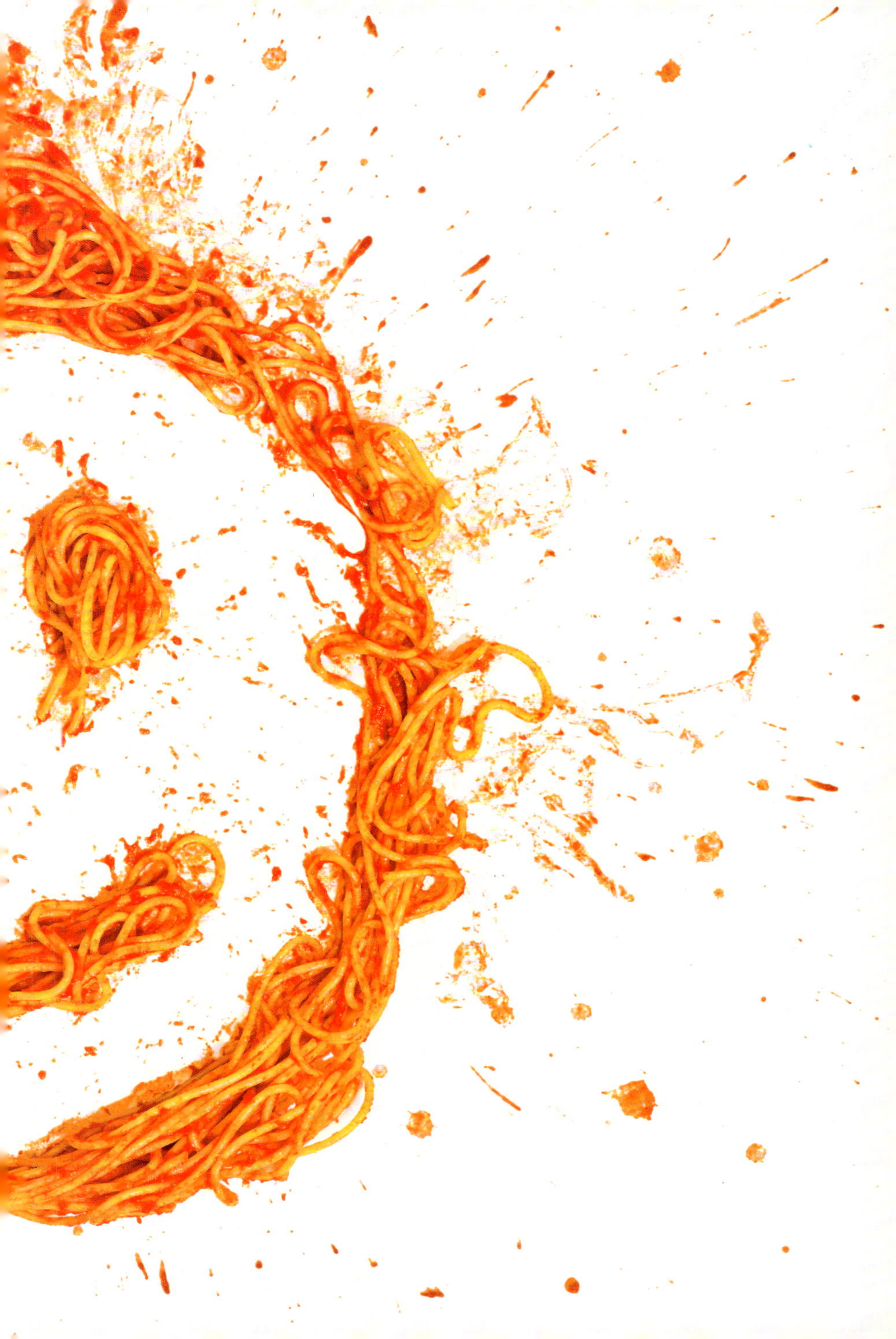

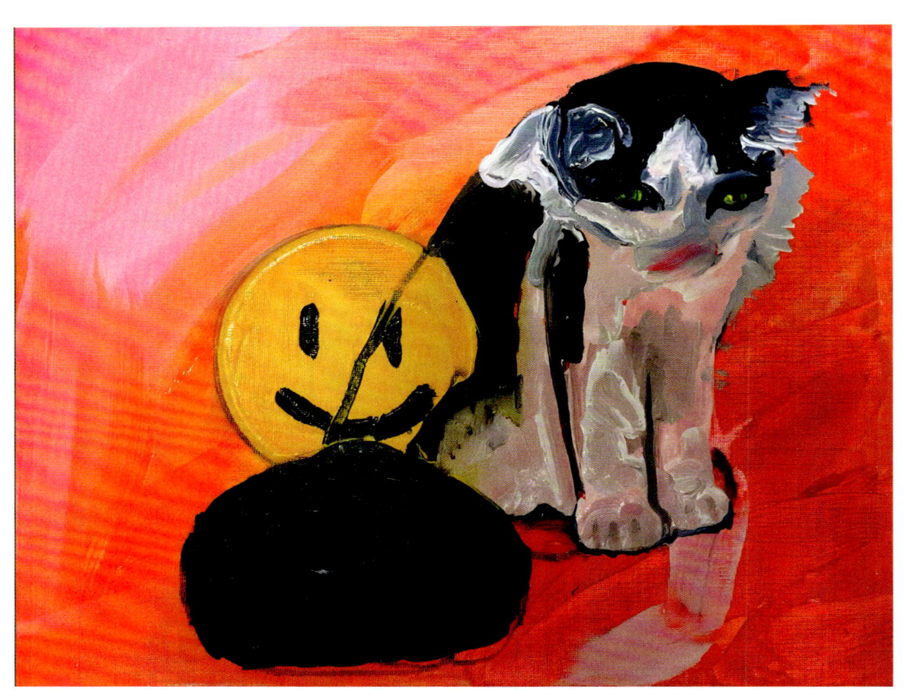

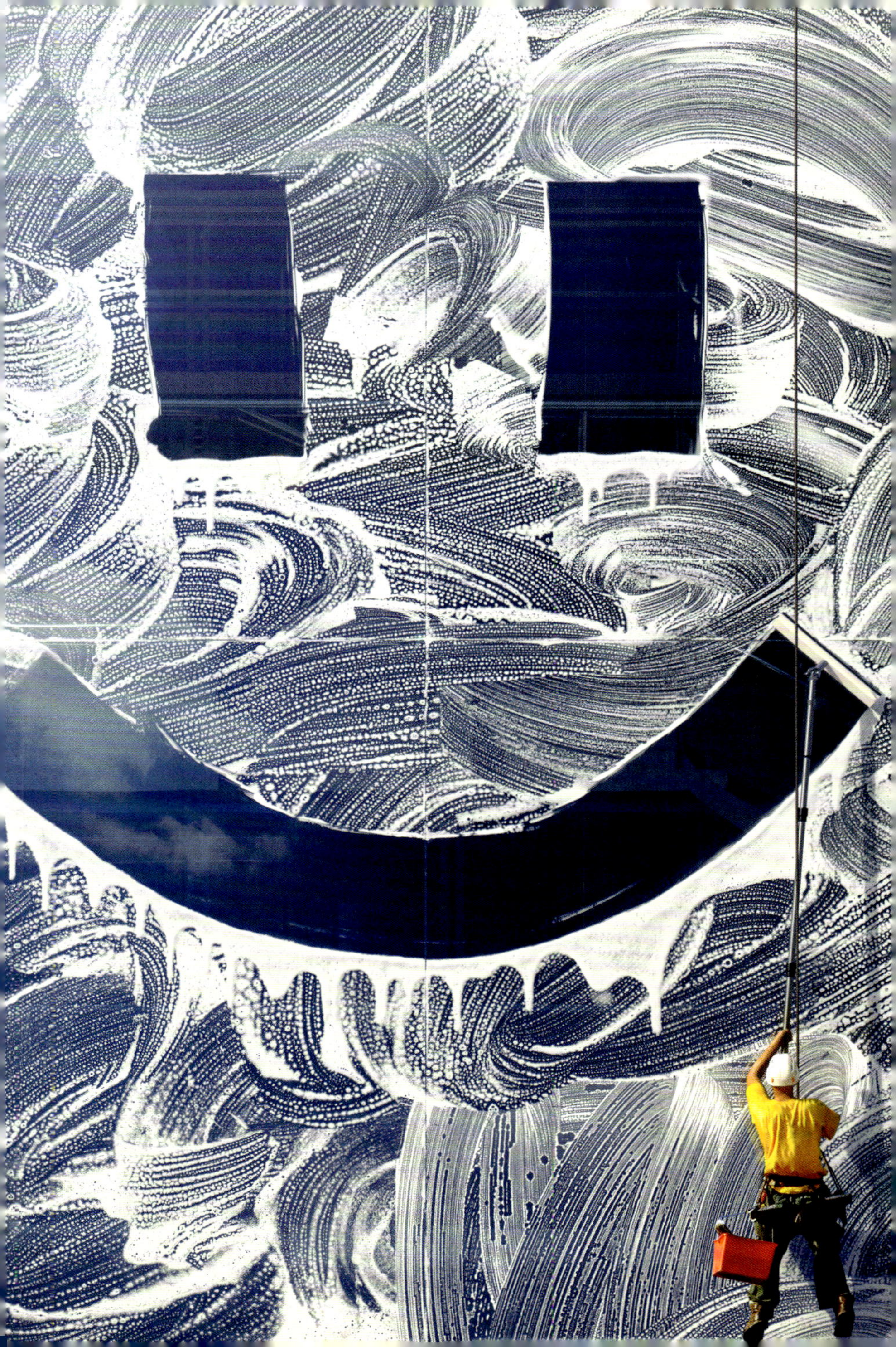

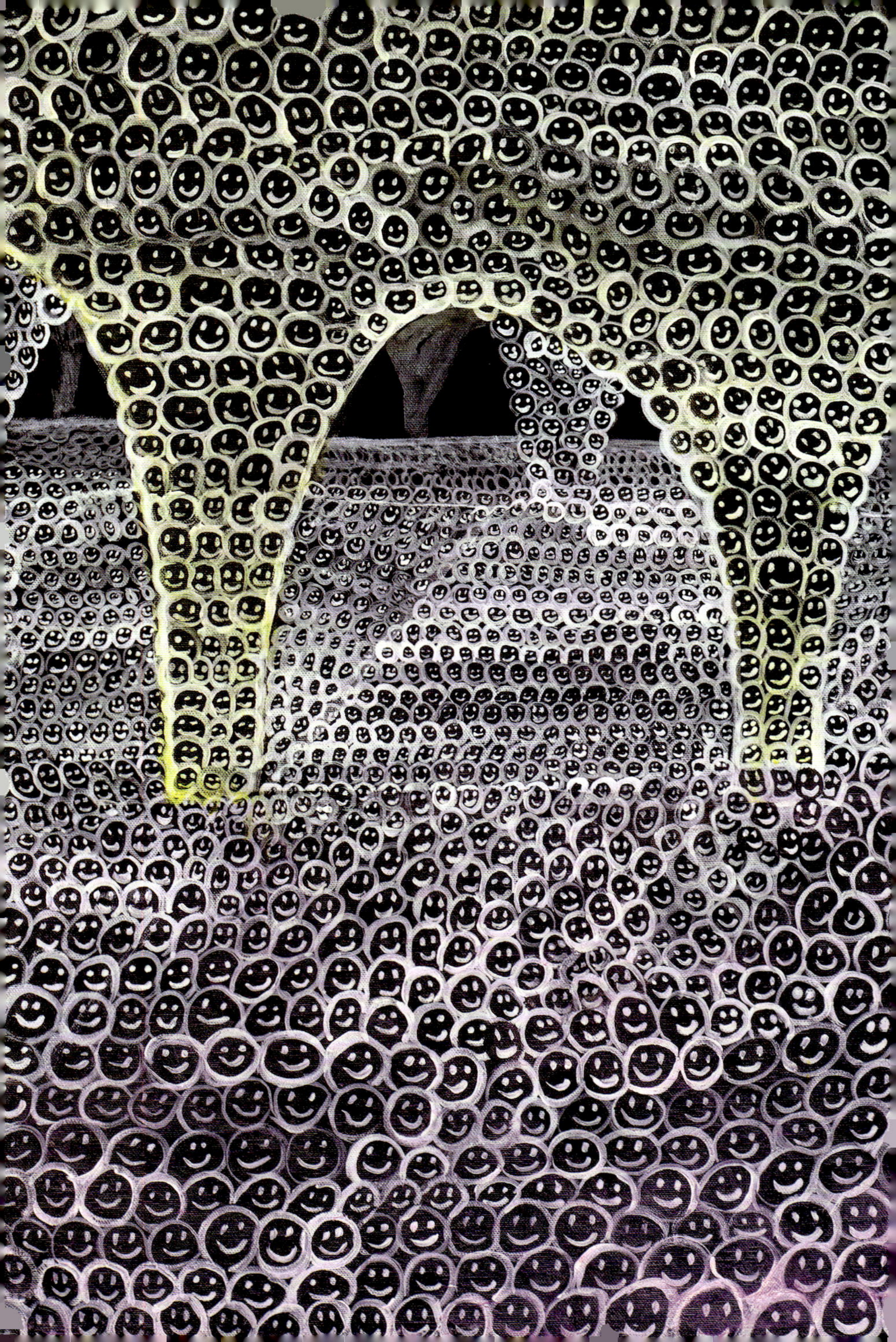

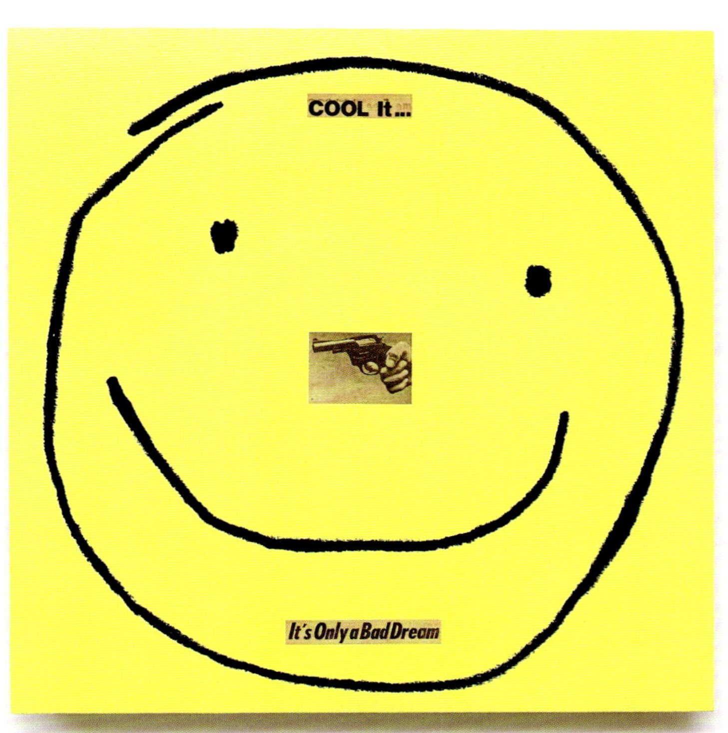

COOL It...
It's Only a Bad Dream

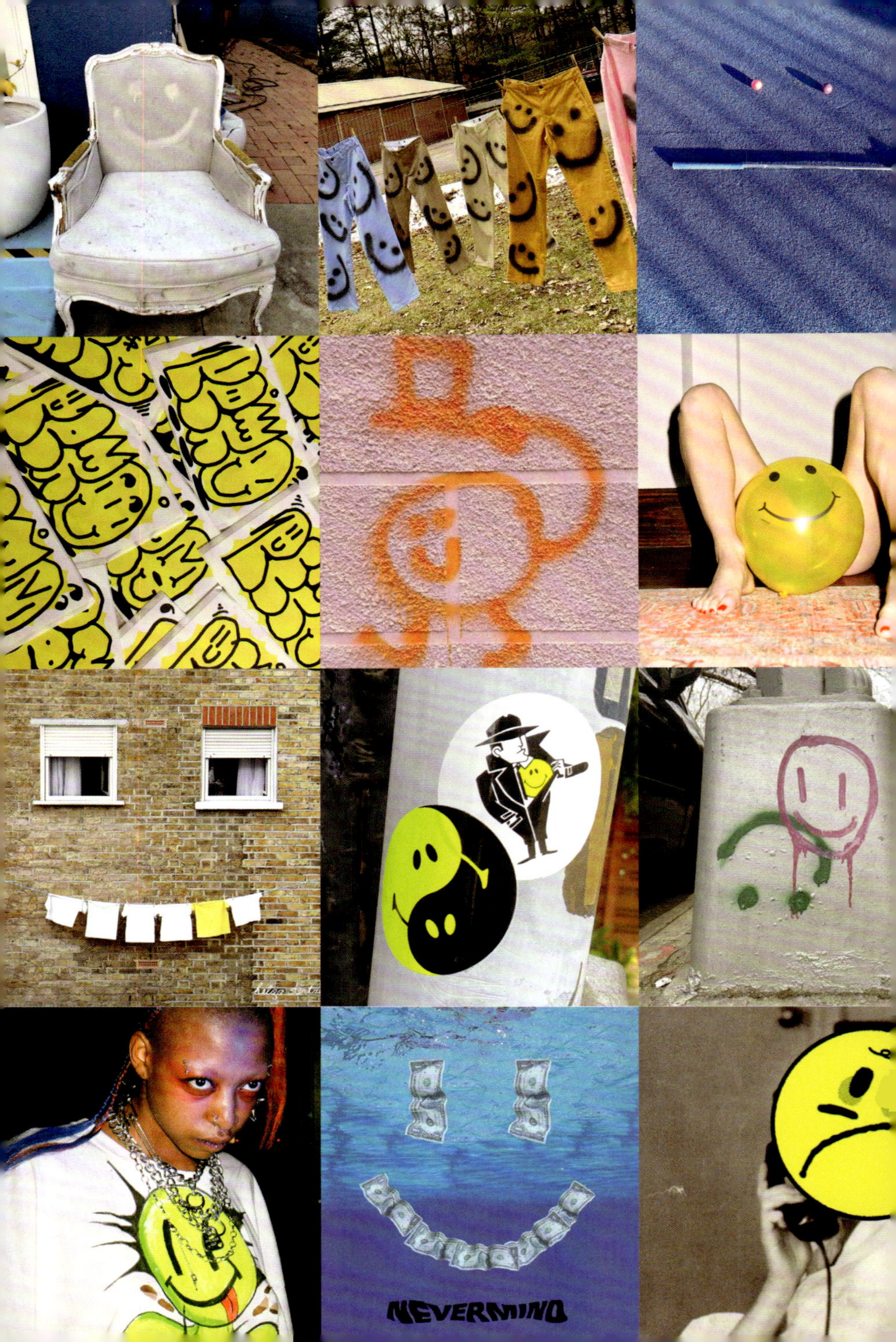
NEVERMIND

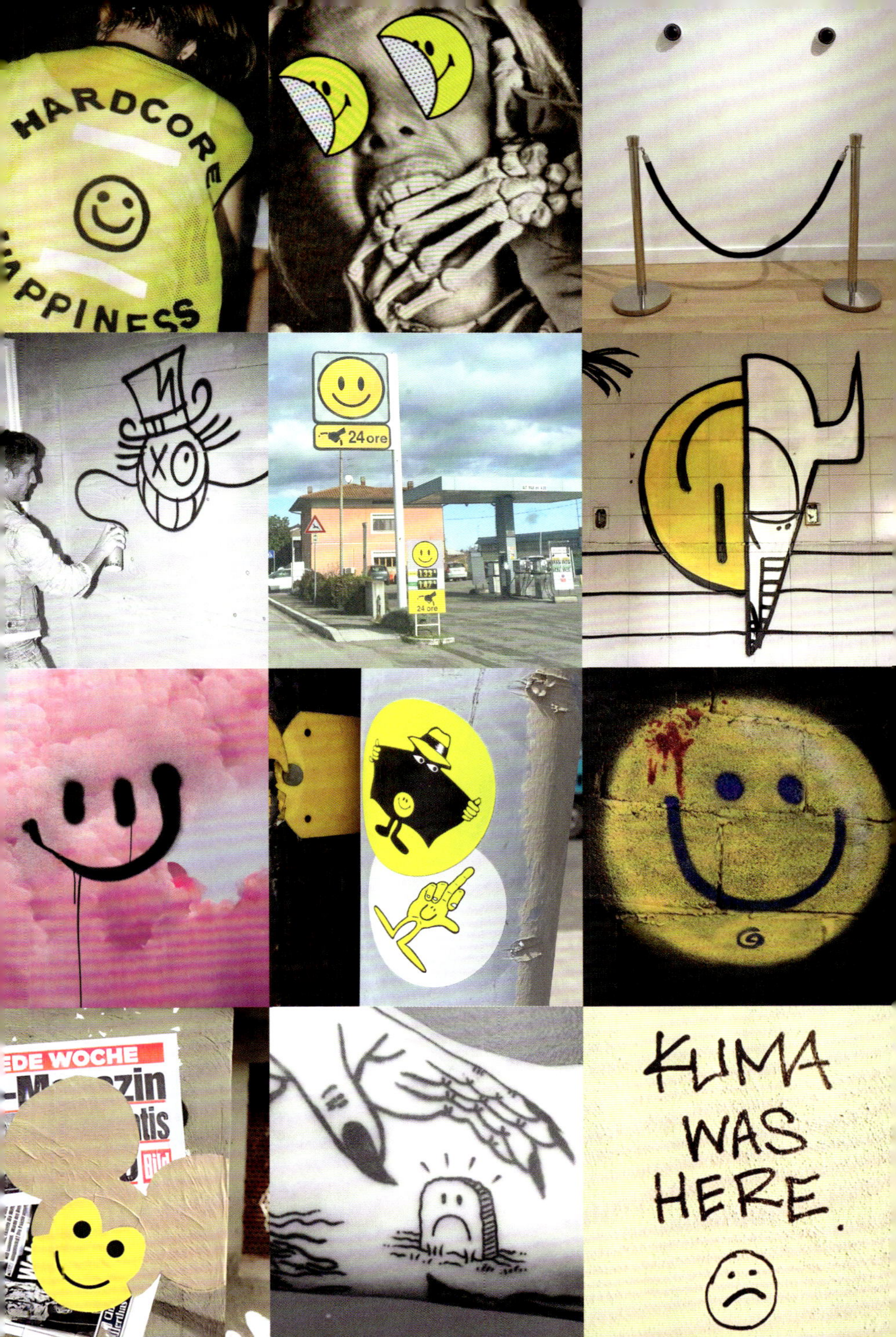
HARDCORE
HAPPINESS
24 ore
24 ore
DE WOCHE
Magazin
atis
Bild
KLIMA
WAS
HERE.

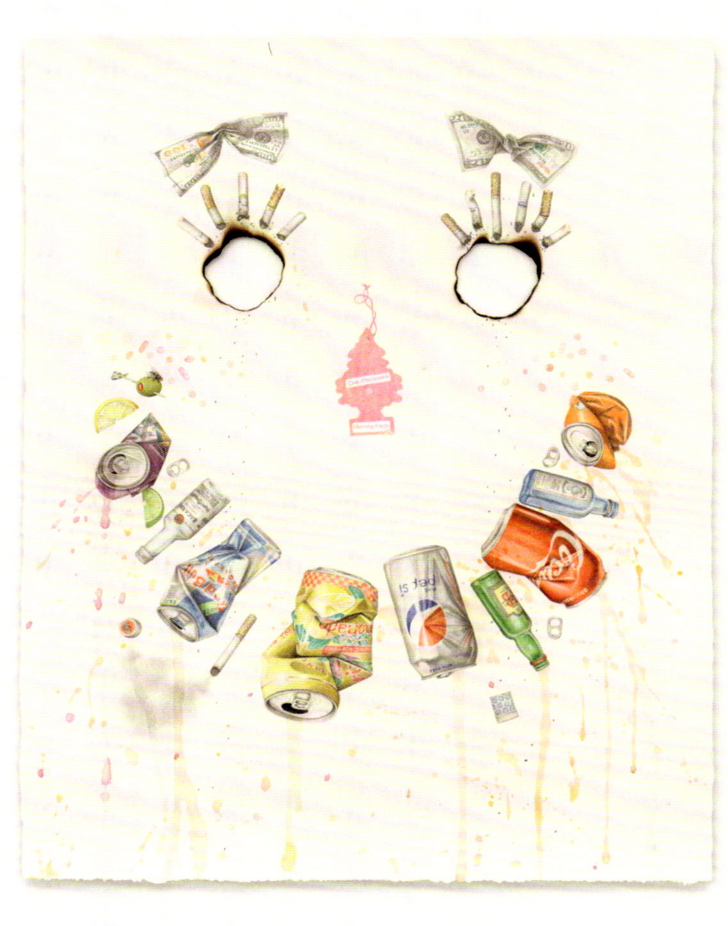

LIVELY
GHOST

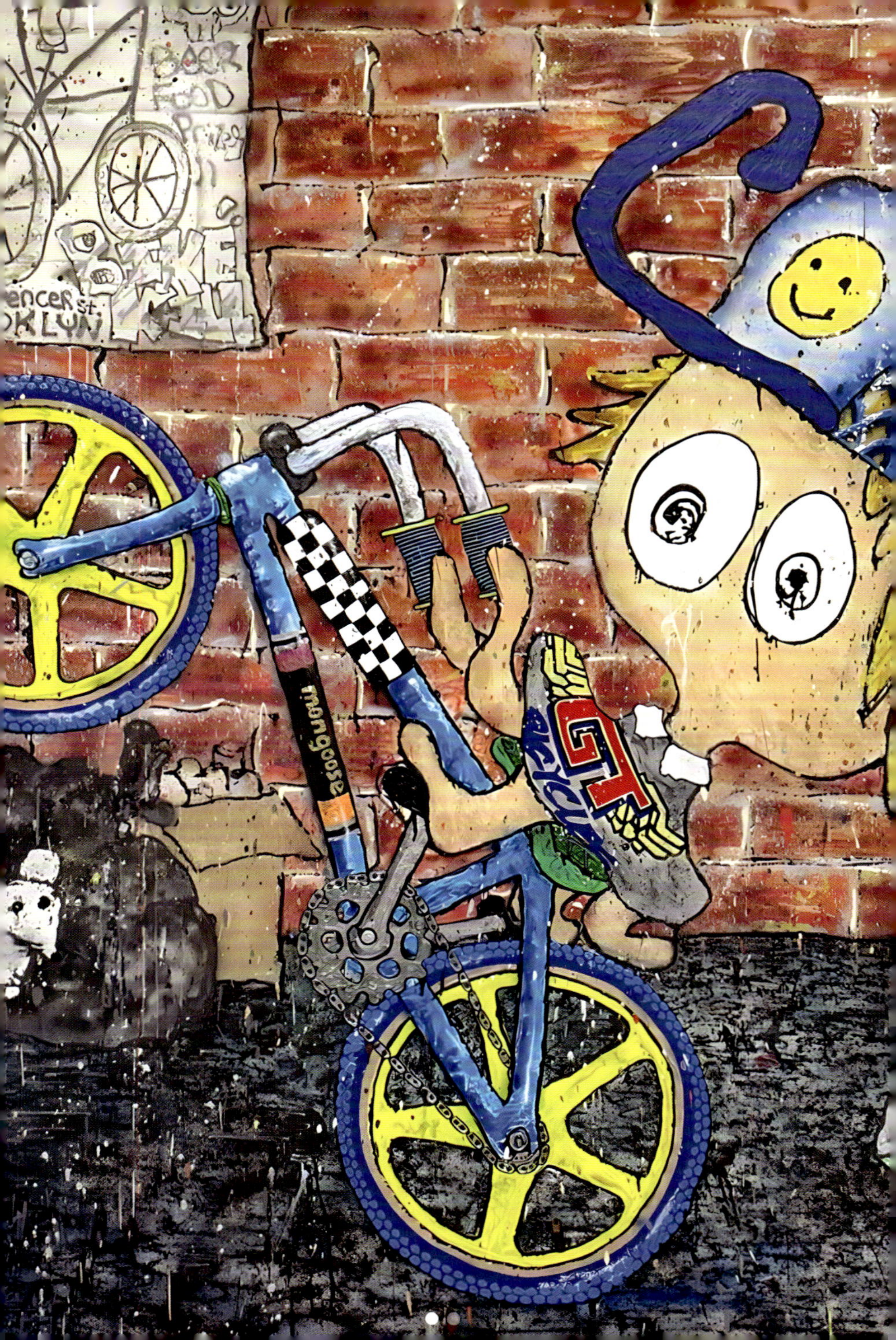

BEER
FOOD
PRIZE
BIKE
encer st.
OKLYN
mongoose
GT

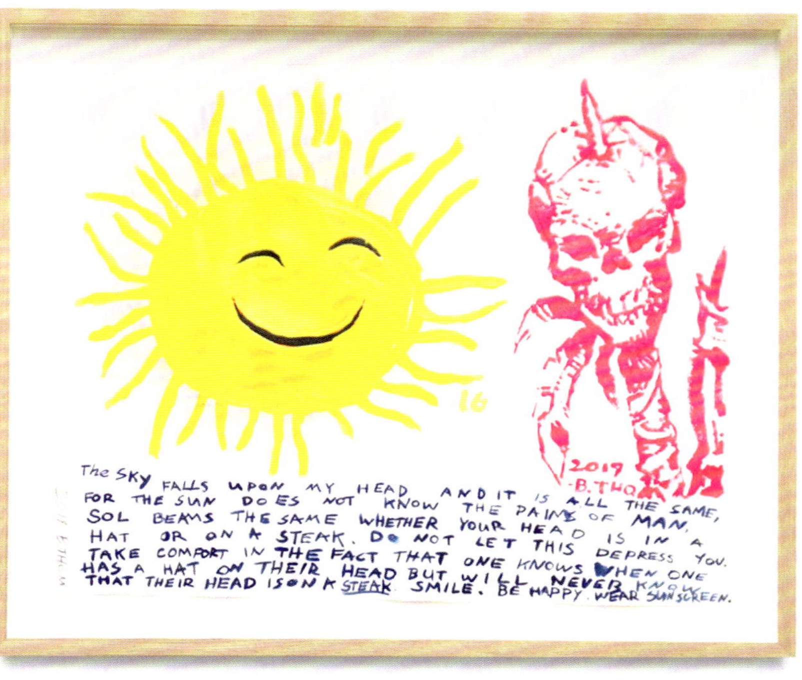
2019
-B. THO
The SKY FALLS UPON MY HEAD AND IT IS ALL THE SAME,
FOR THE SUN DOES NOT KNOW THE PAINE OF MAN,
SOL BEAMS THE SAME WHETHER YOUR HEAD IS IN A
HAT OR ON A STEAK. DO NOT LET THIS DEPRESS YOU.
TAKE COMFORT IN THE FACT THAT ONE KNOWS WHEN ONE
HAS A HAT ON THEIR HEAD BUT WILL NEVER KNOW
THAT THEIR HEAD IS ON A STEAK. SMILE. BE HAPPY. WEAR SUNSCREEN.

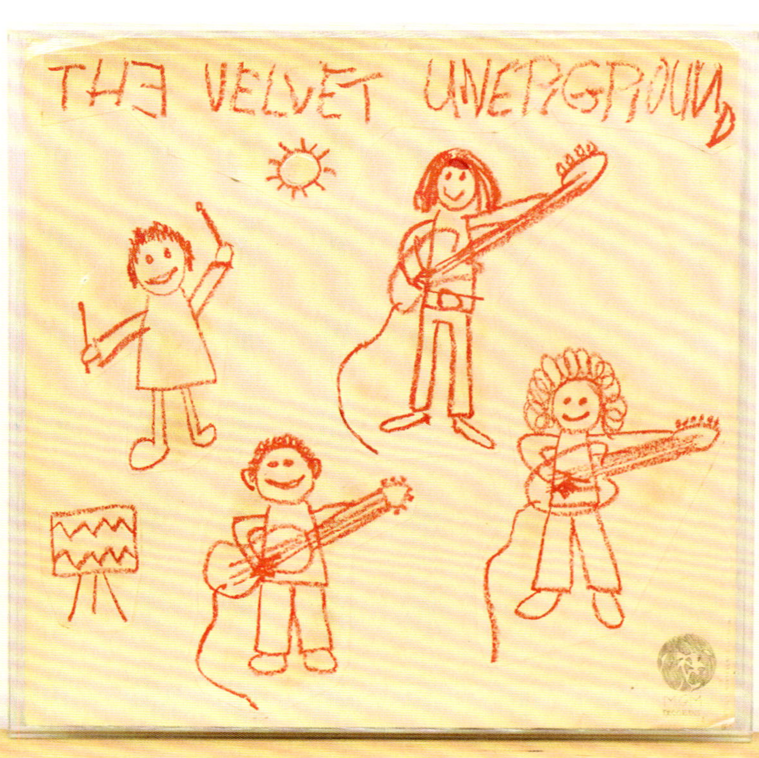
THE VELVET UNDERGROUND

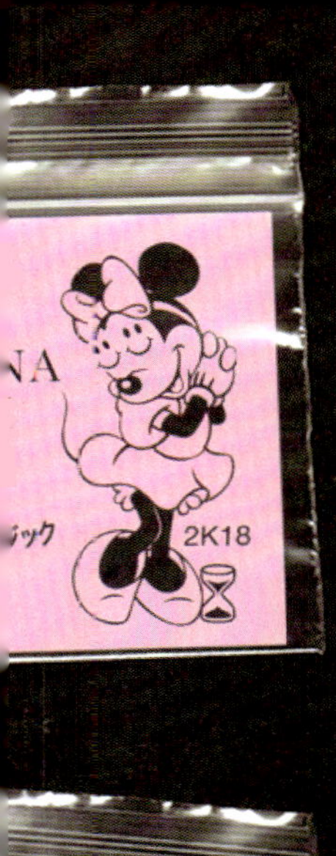
NA
ジック
2K18

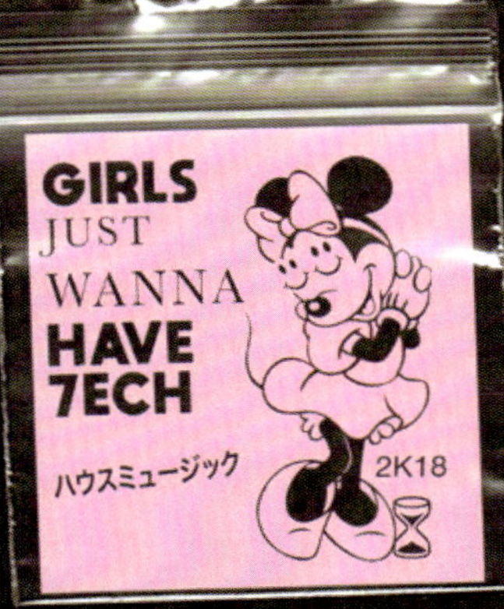
GIRLS
JUST
WANNA
HAVE
7ECH
ハウスミュージック
2K18

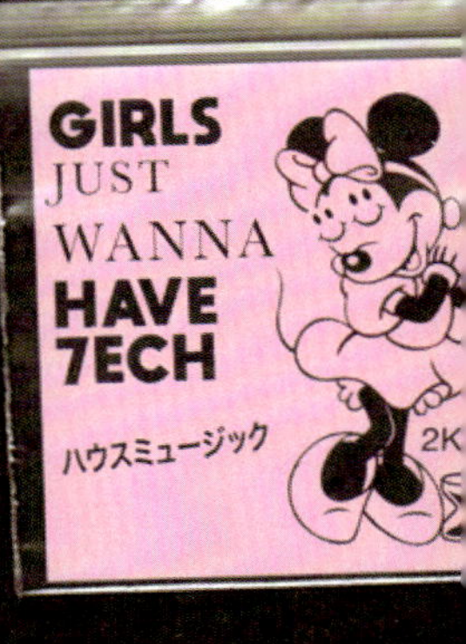
GIRLS
JUST
WANNA
HAVE
7ECH
ハウスミュージック
2K

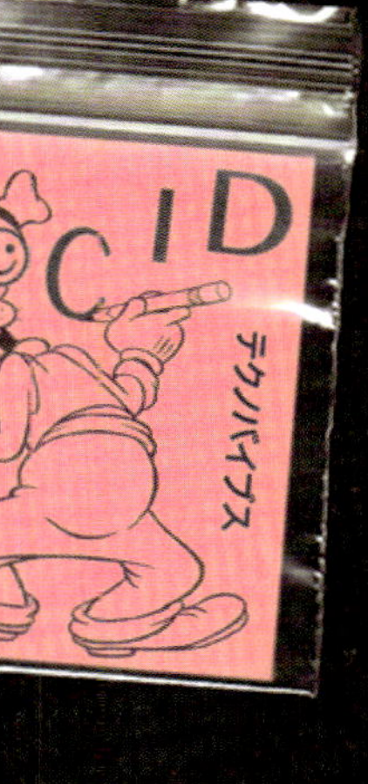
C D
テクノハウス

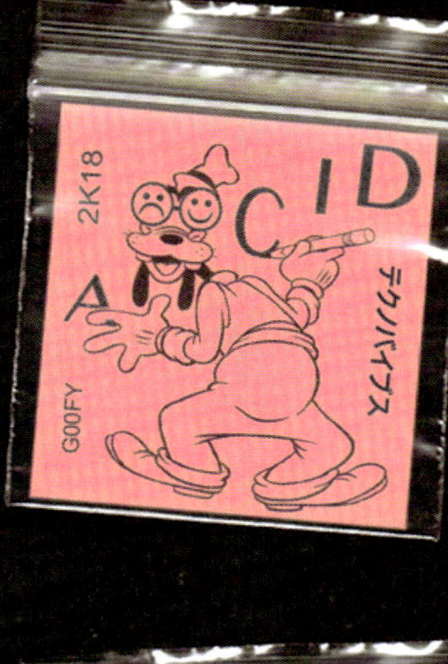
2K18
ACID
GOOFY
テクノハウス

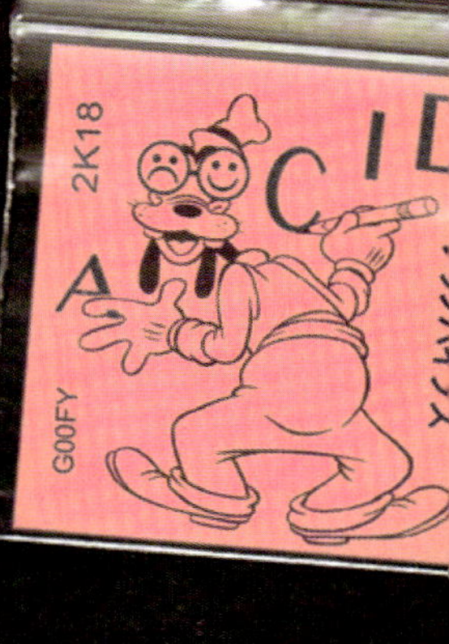
2K18
ACID
GOOFY
C D

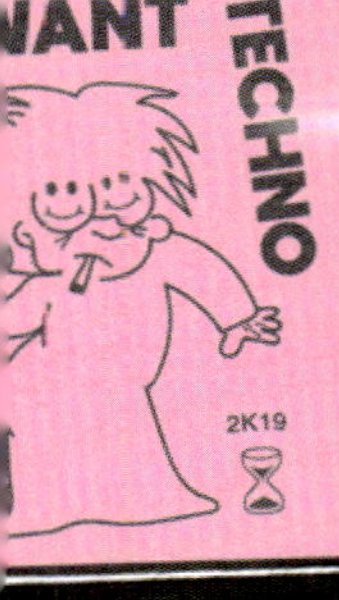
WANT
TECHNO
2K19

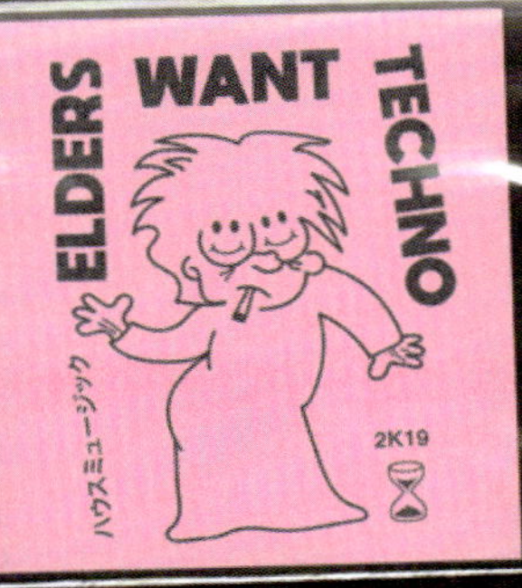
ELDERS WANT
TECHNO
ハウスミュージック
2K19

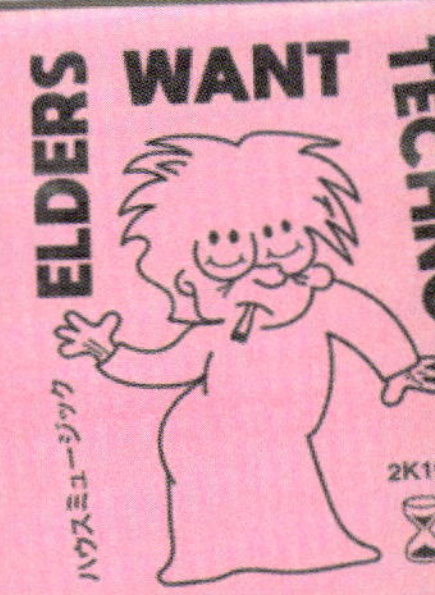
ELDERS WANT
TECHNO
2K19

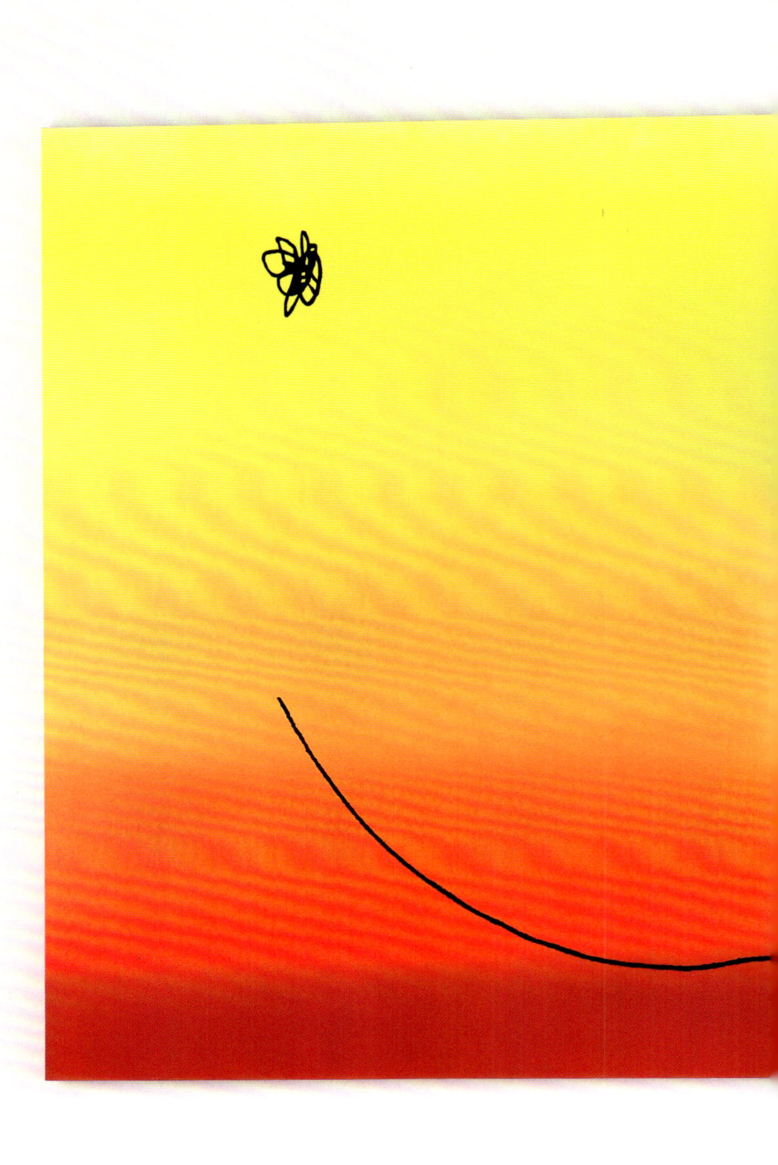

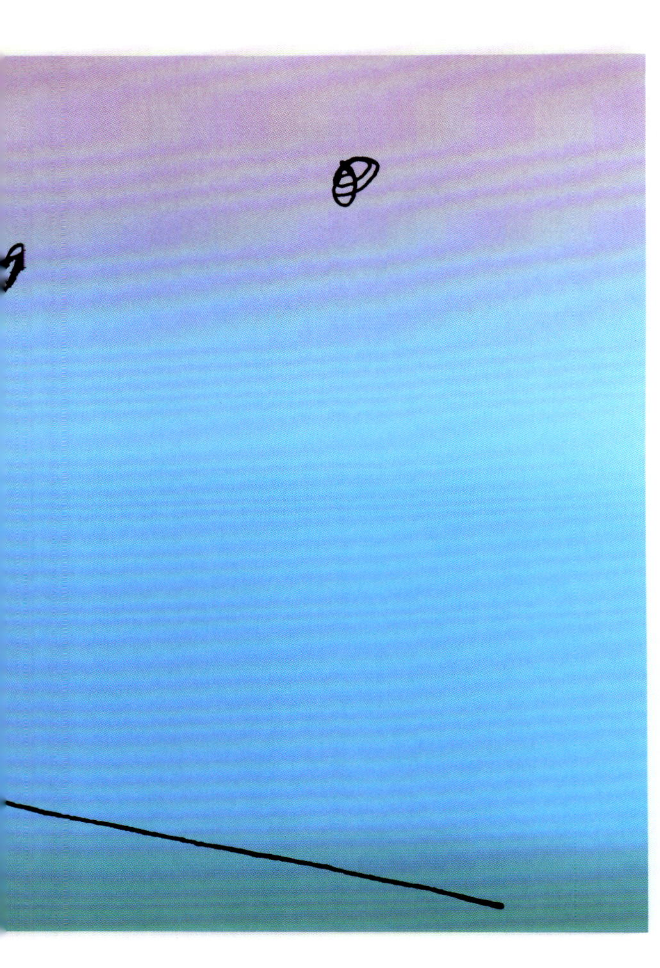

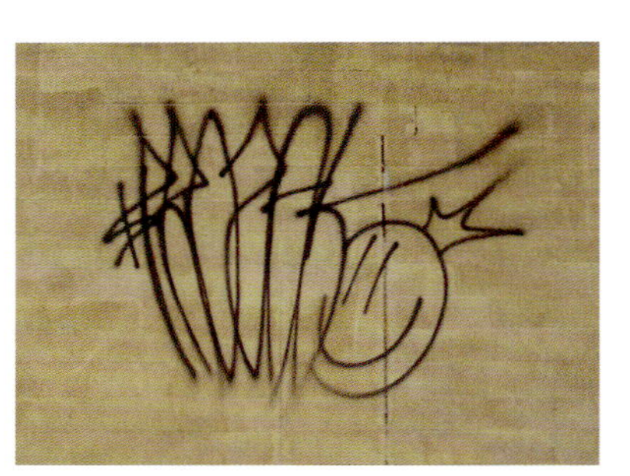

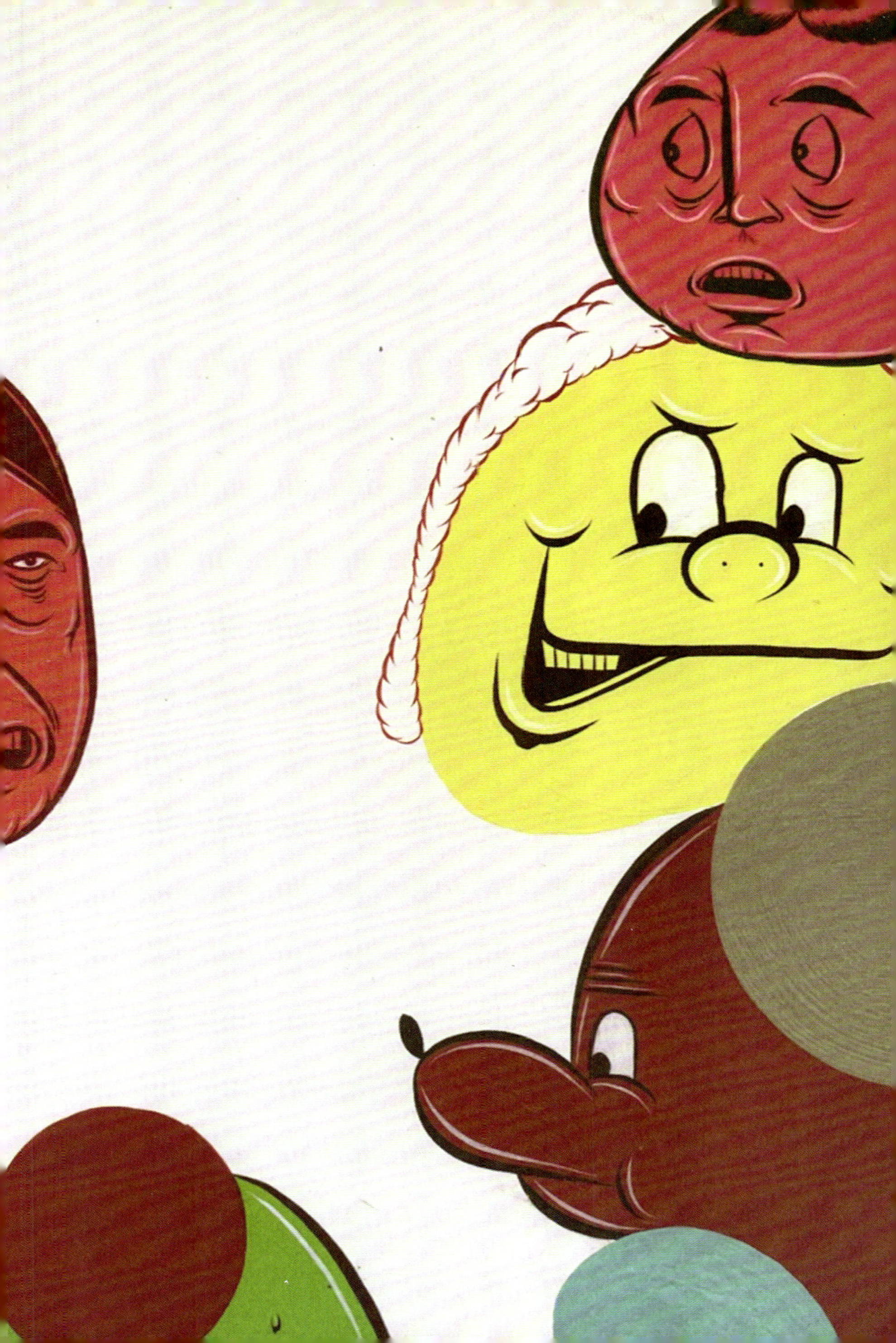

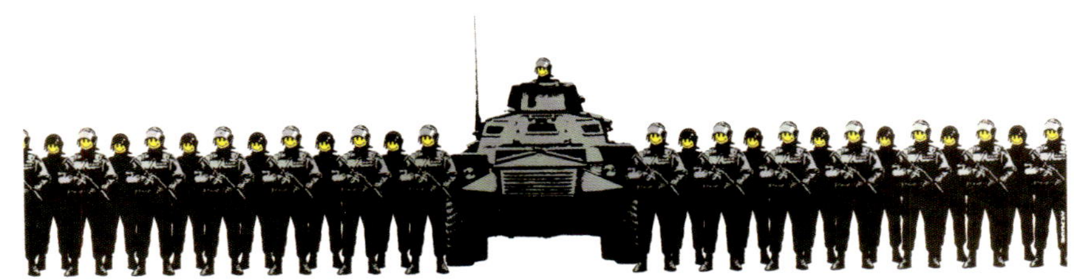

Have A Nice Day

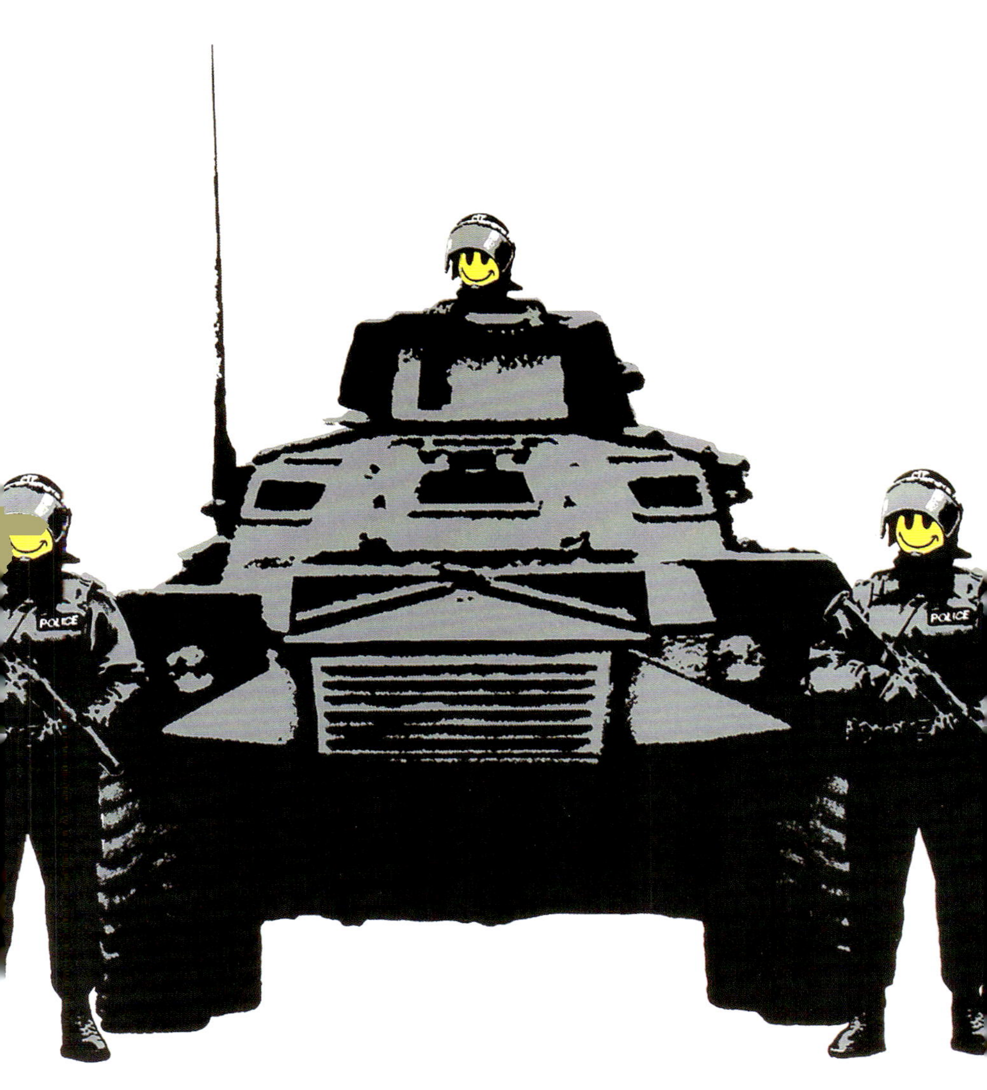

Have A Nice Day

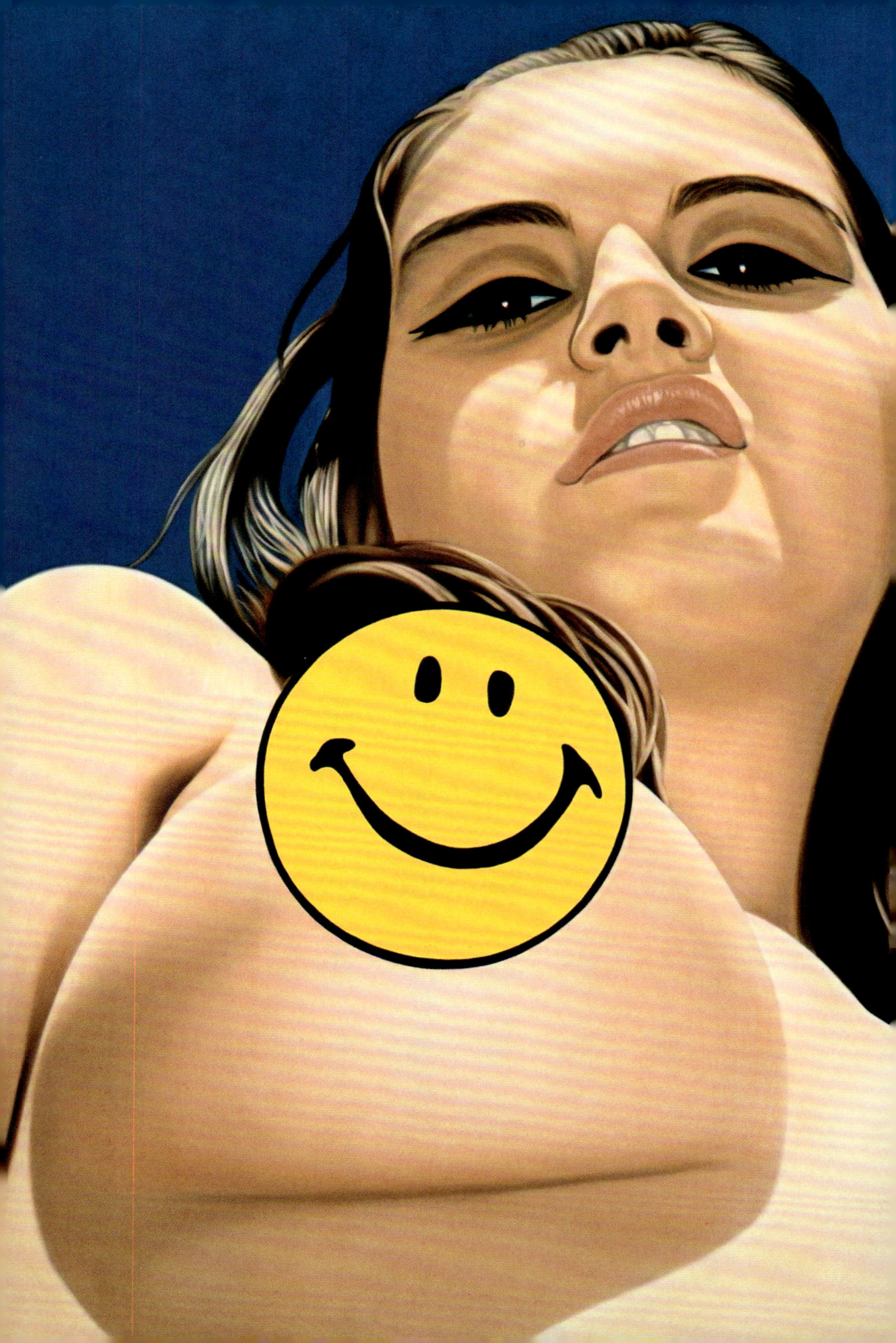

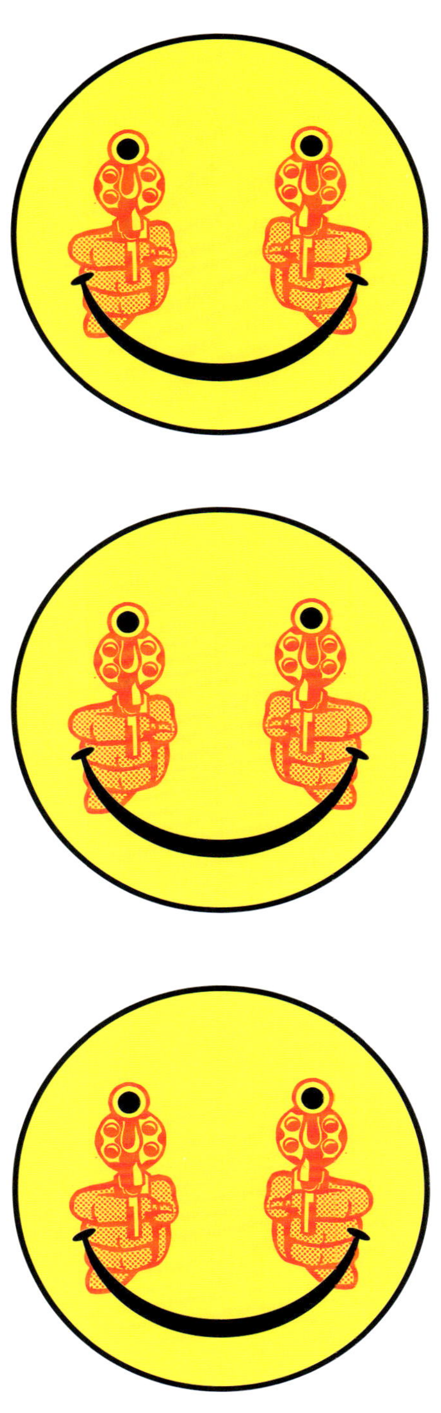

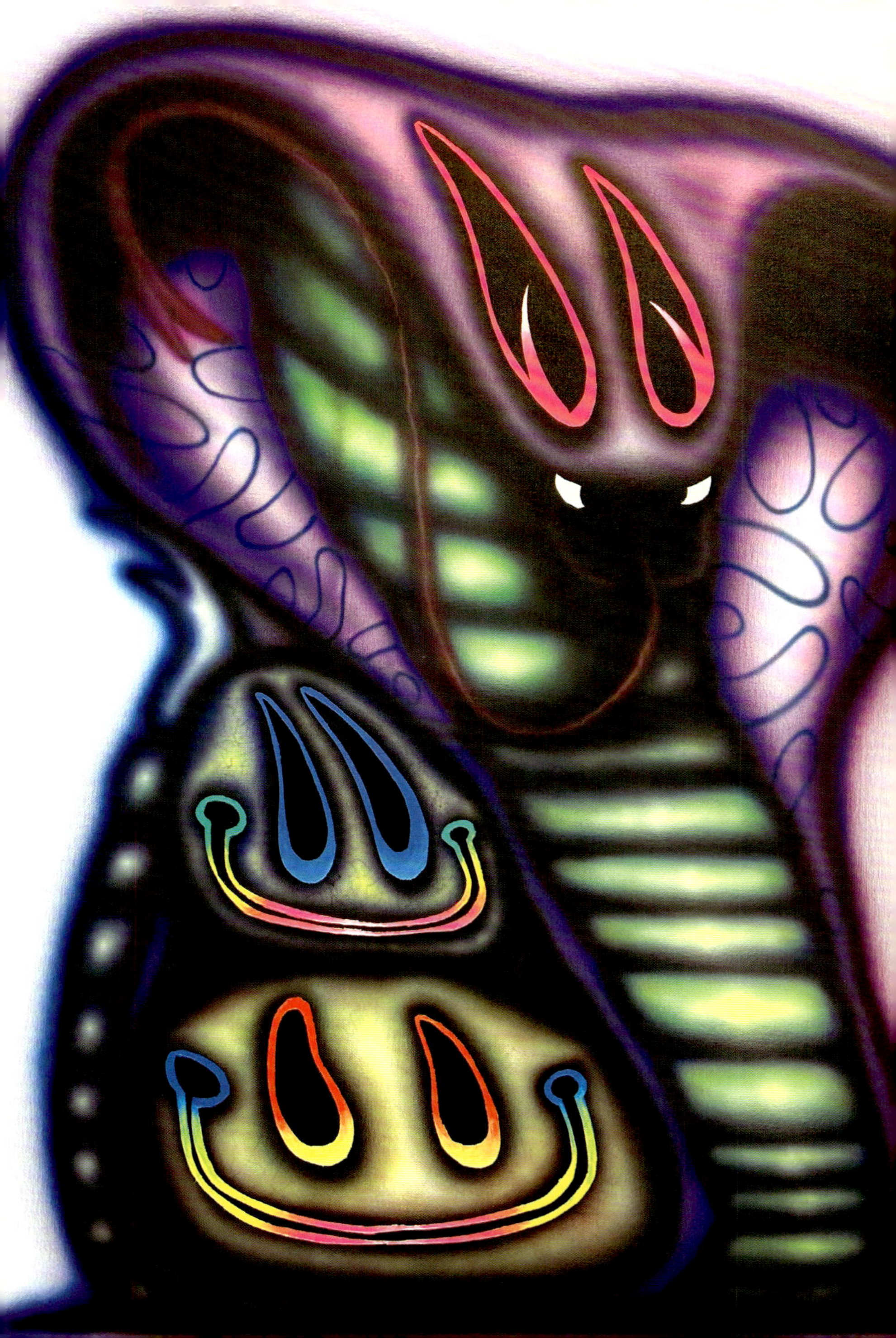

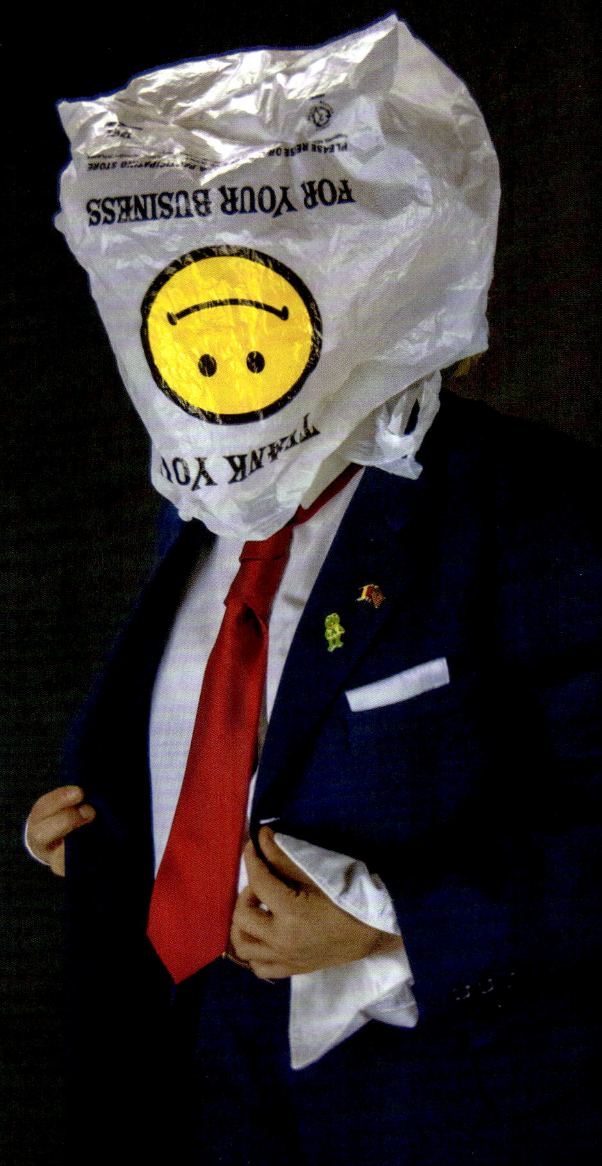

FOR YOUR BUSINESS
PLEASE RETURN TO A PARTICIPATING STORE
THANK YOU

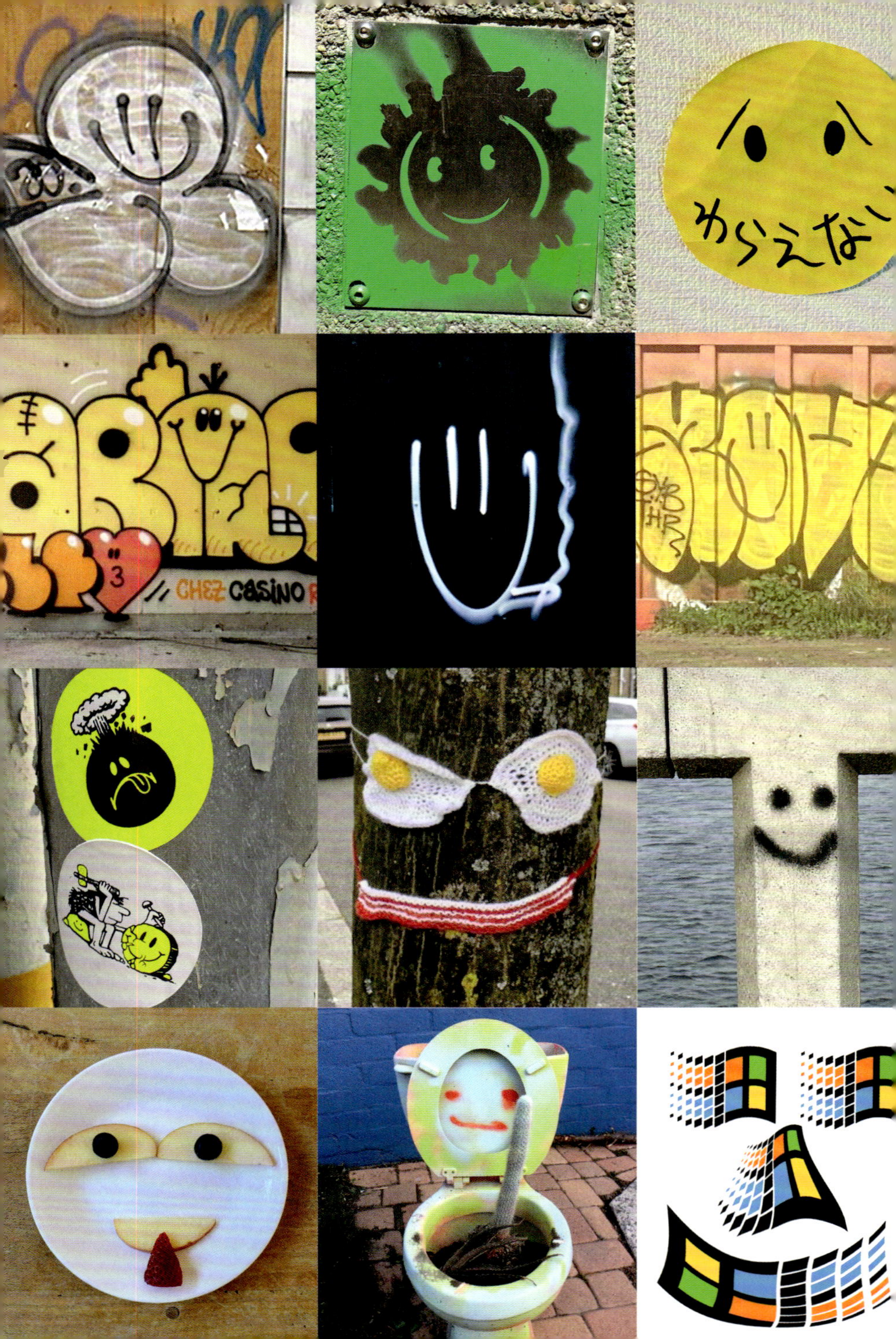
わらえない
CHEZ CASINO R

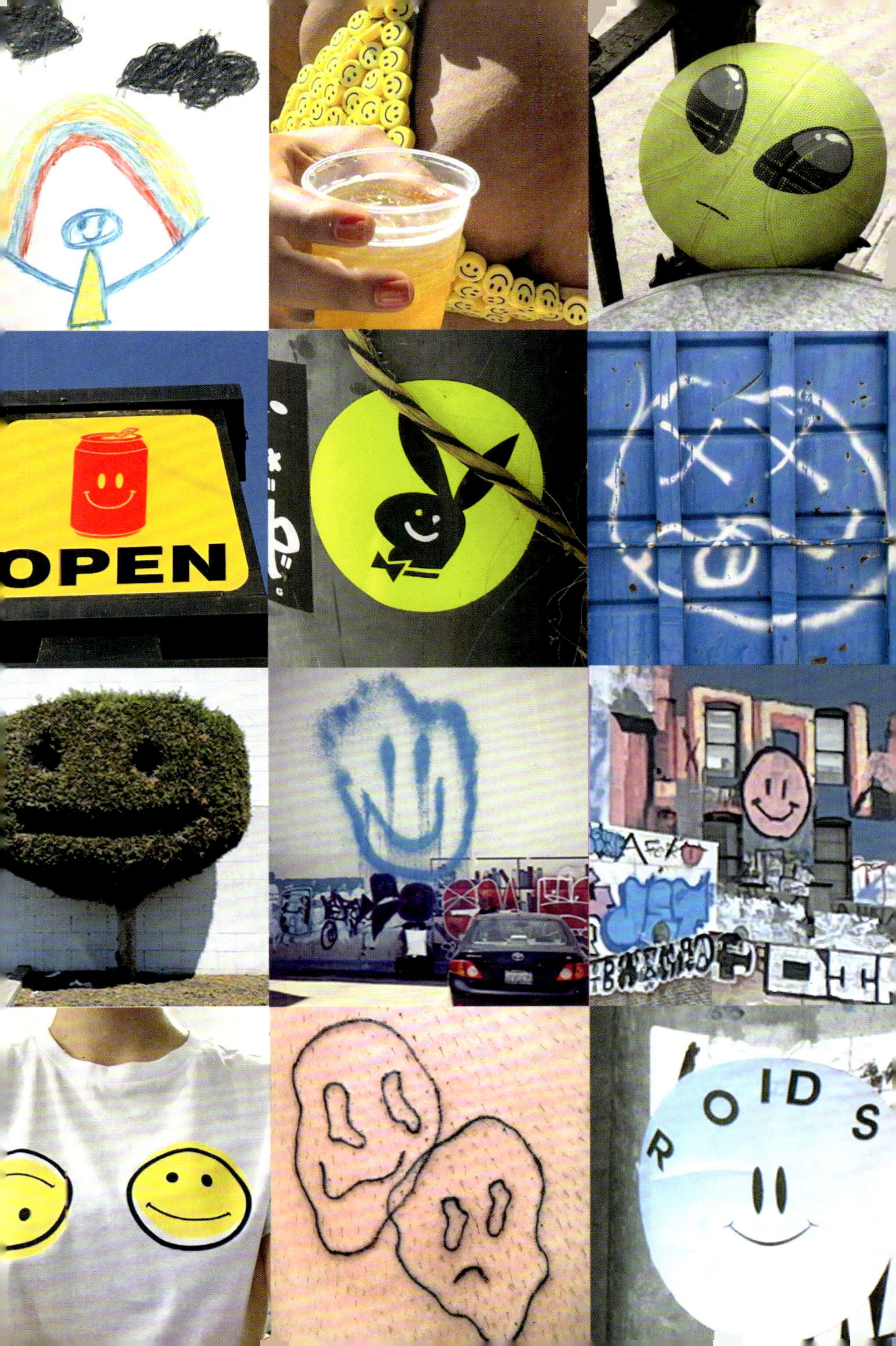

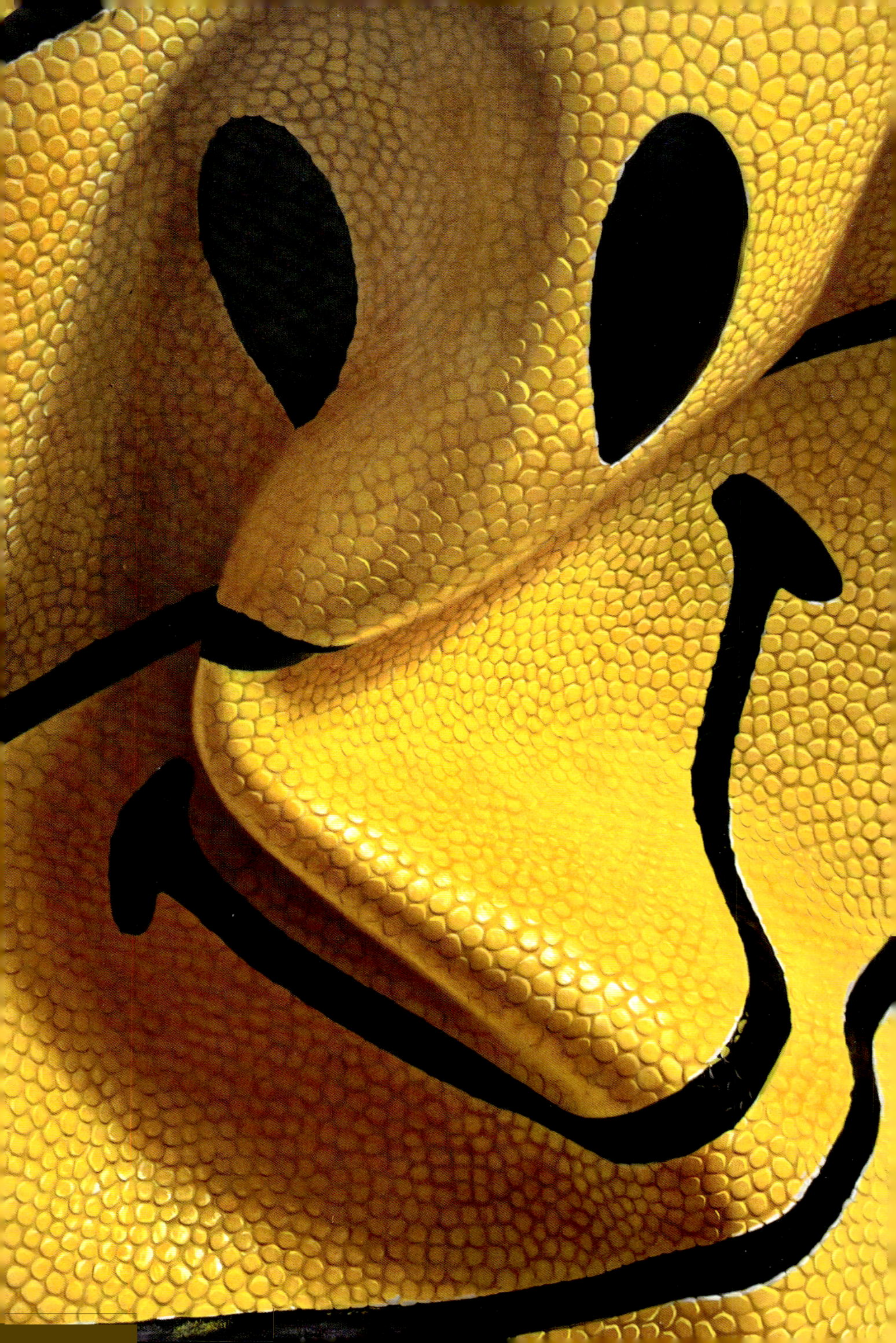

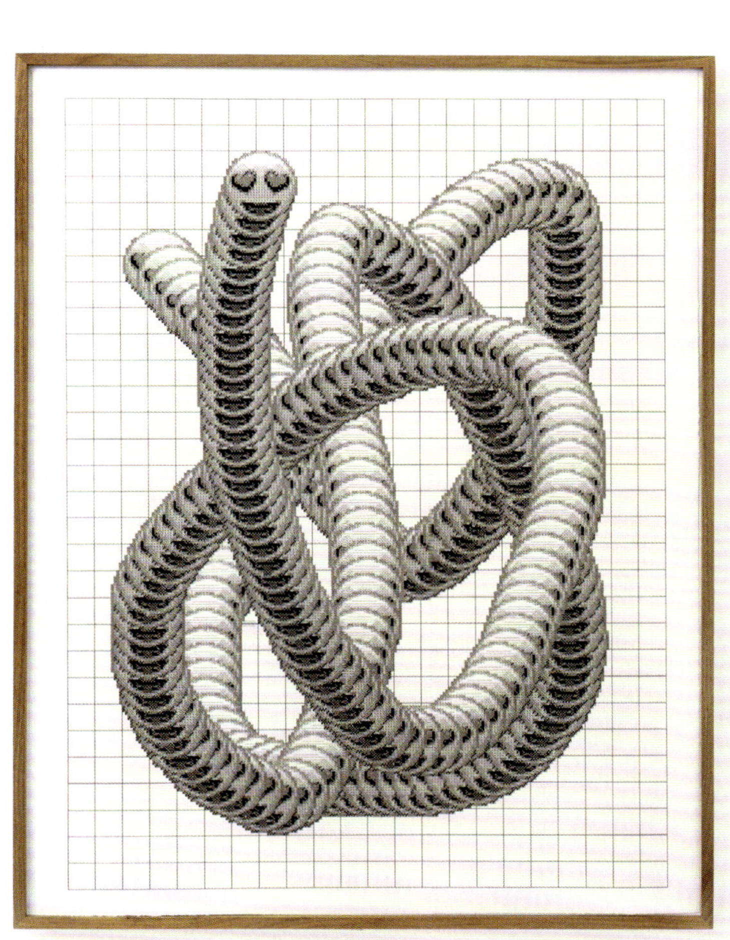

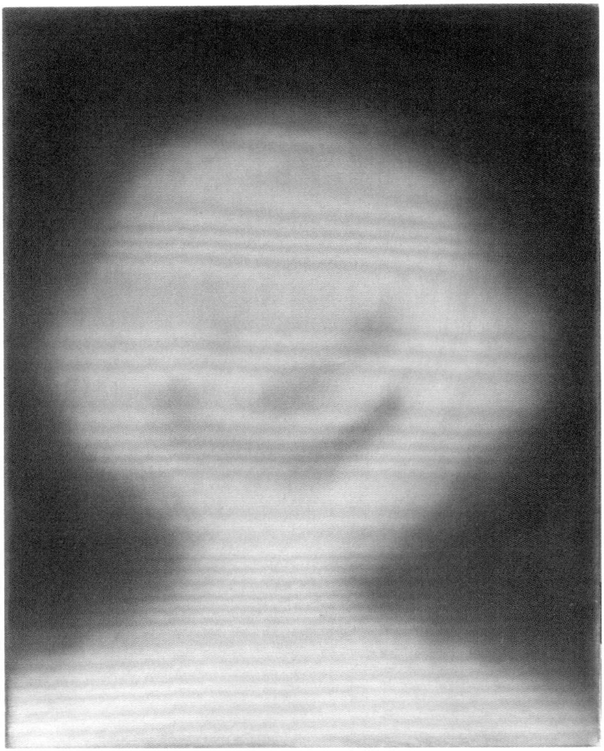

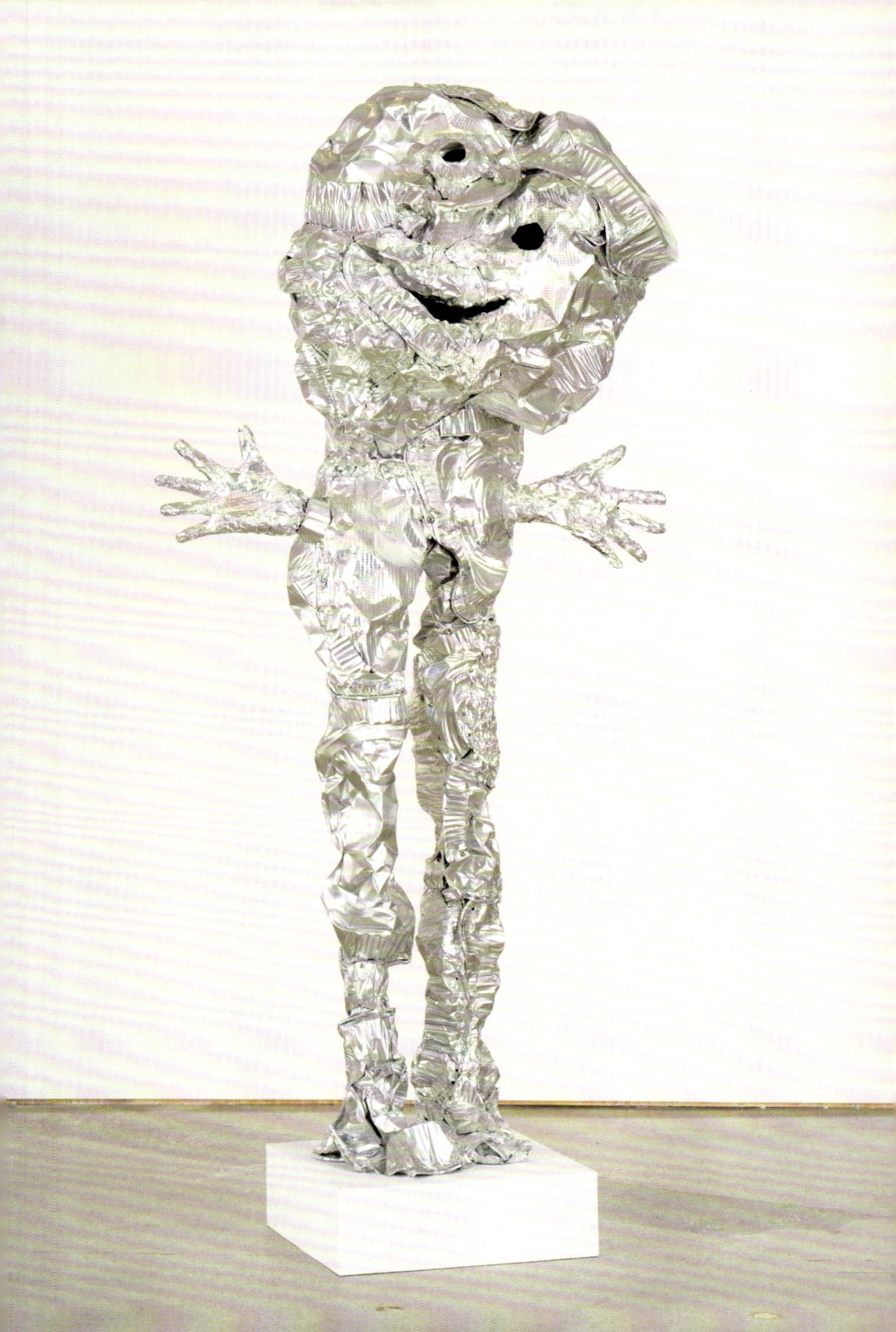

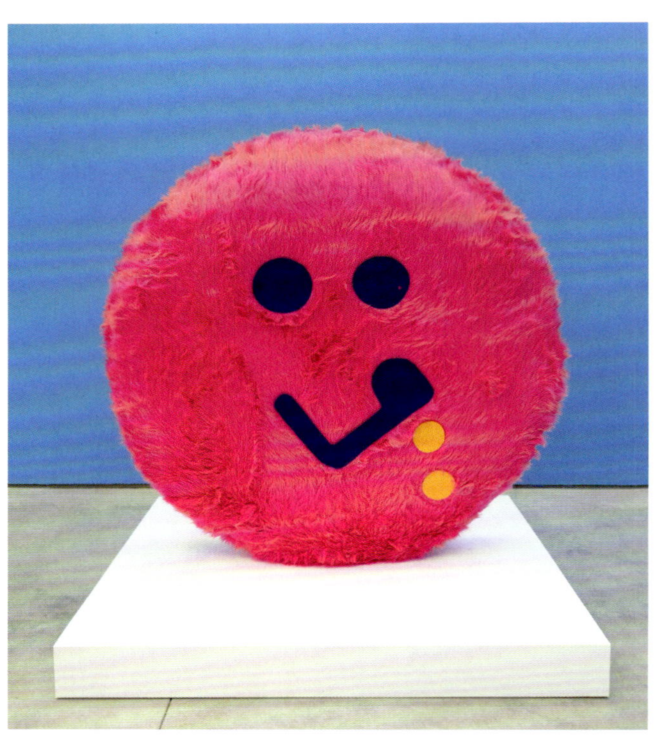

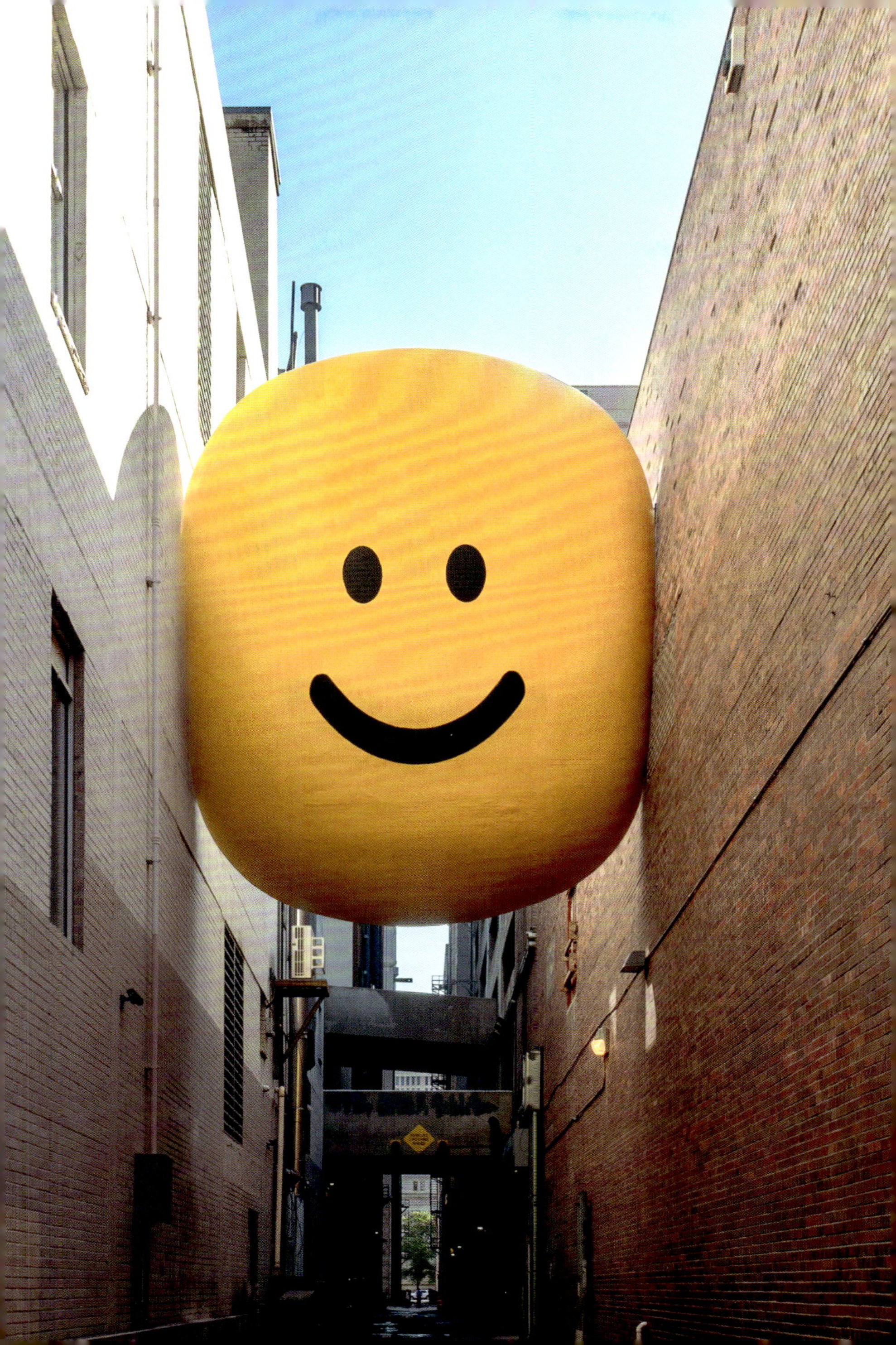

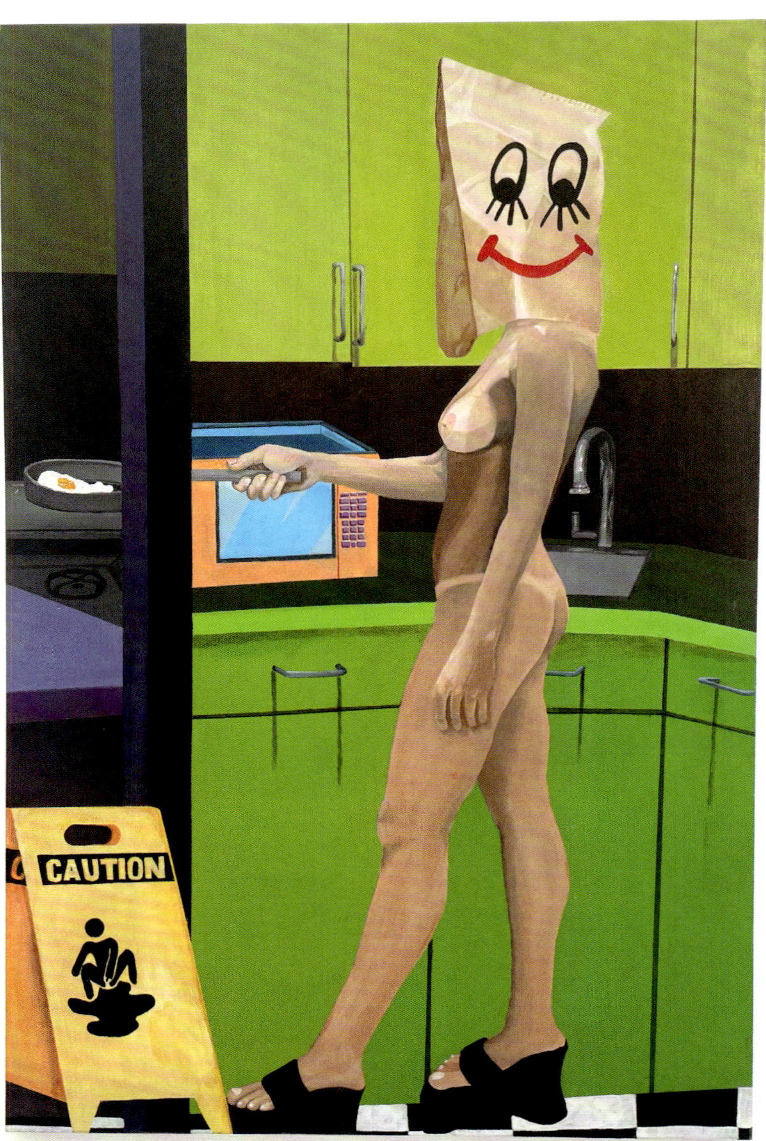
CAUTION

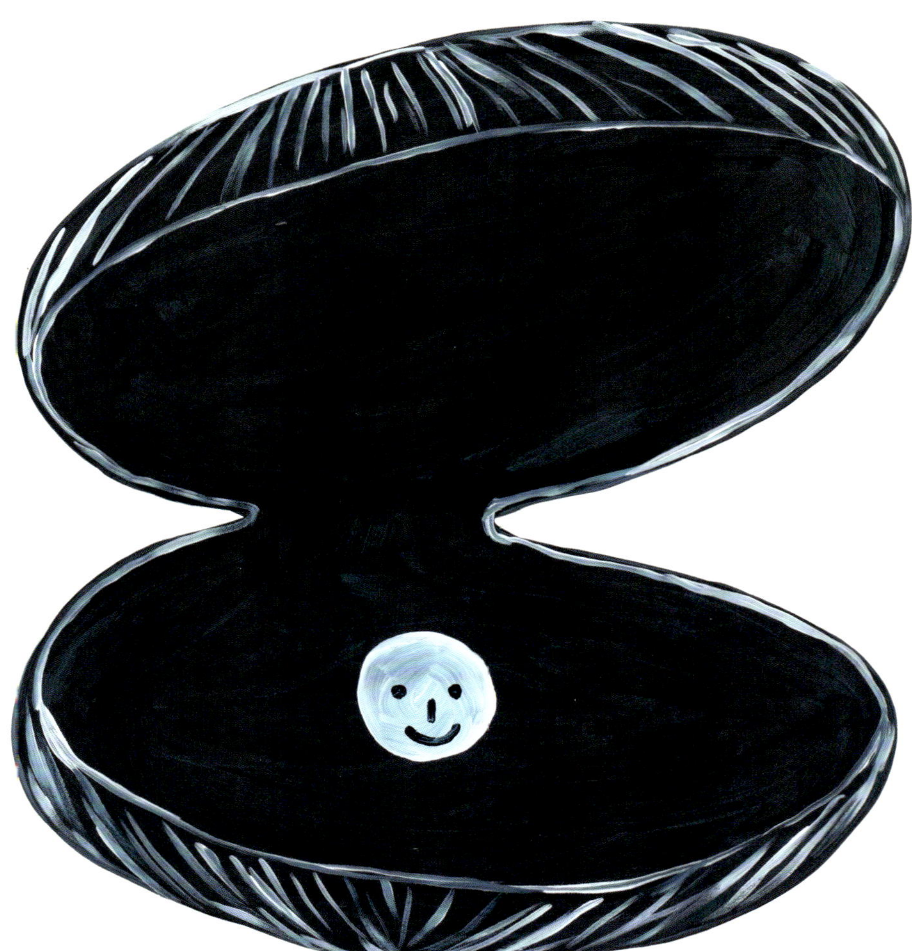

YOU ARE
SPECIAL

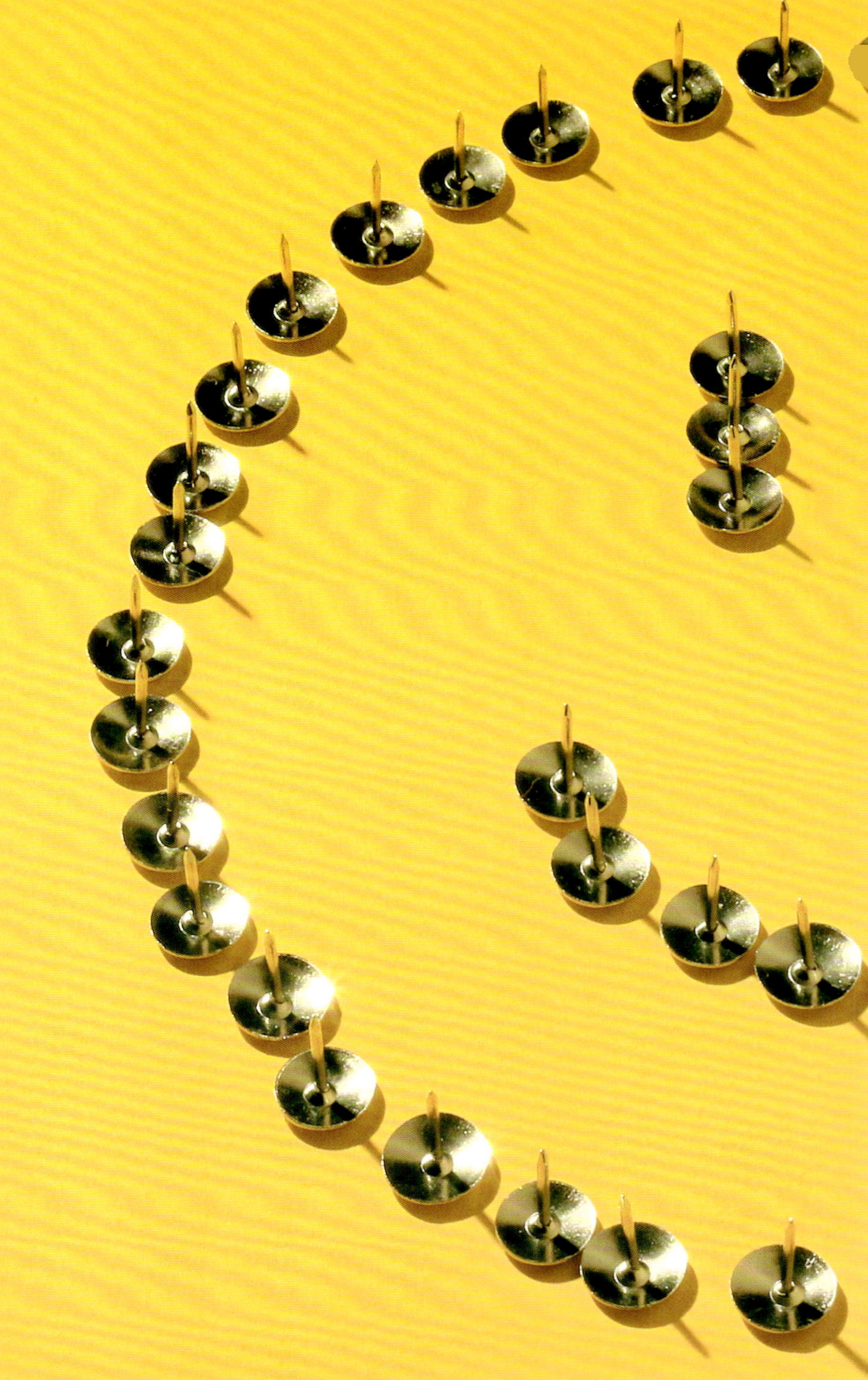

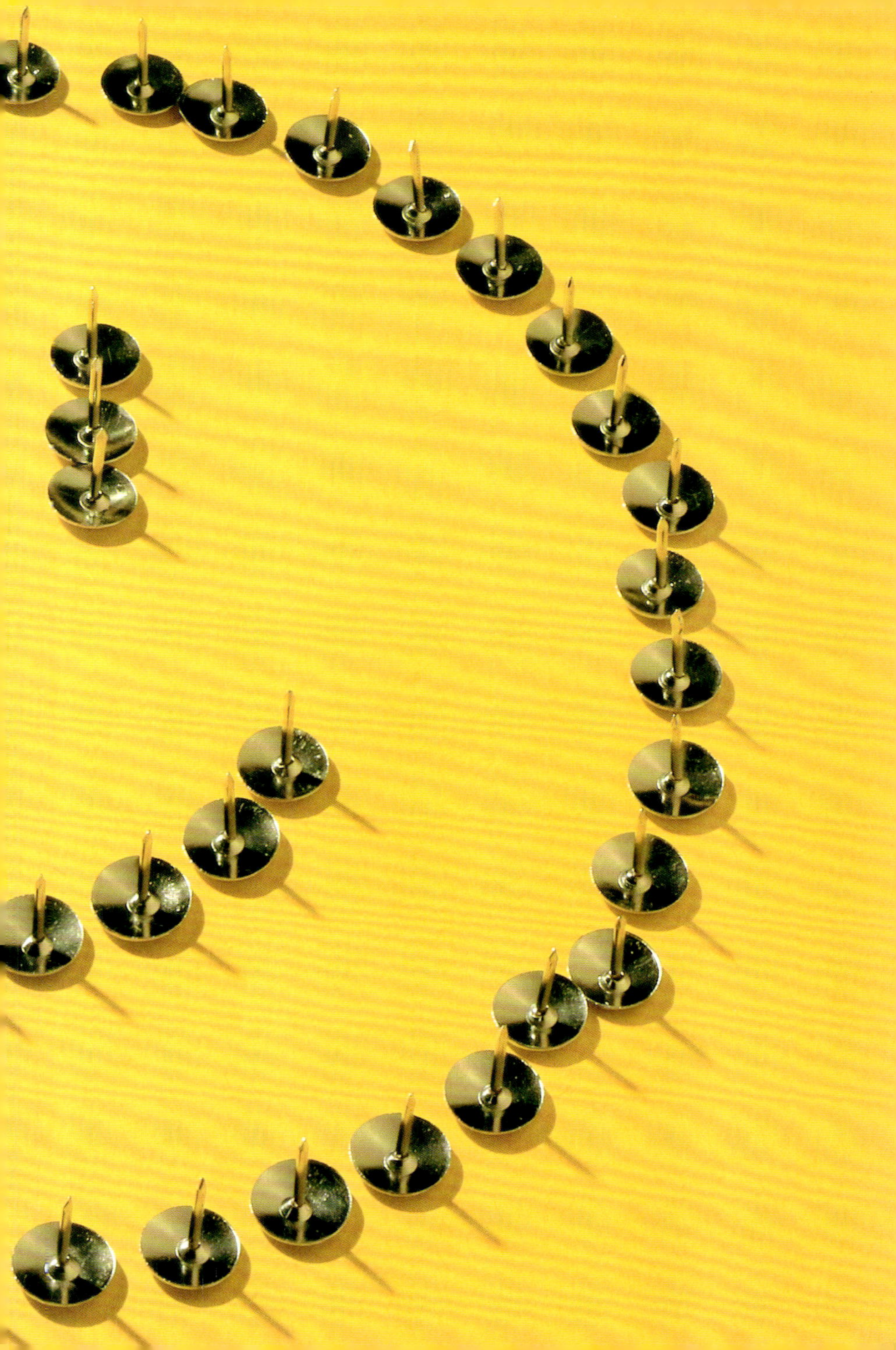

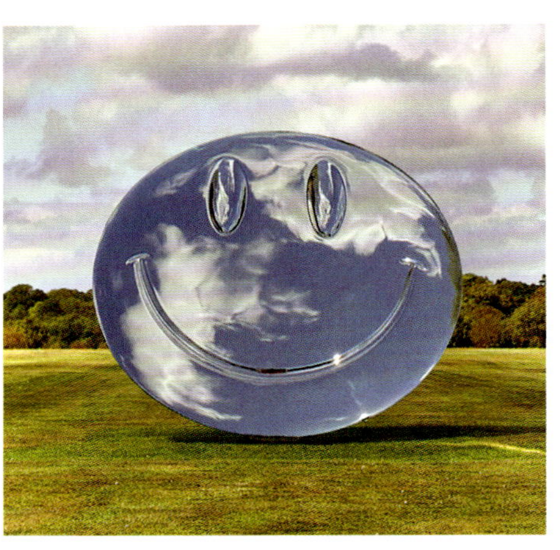

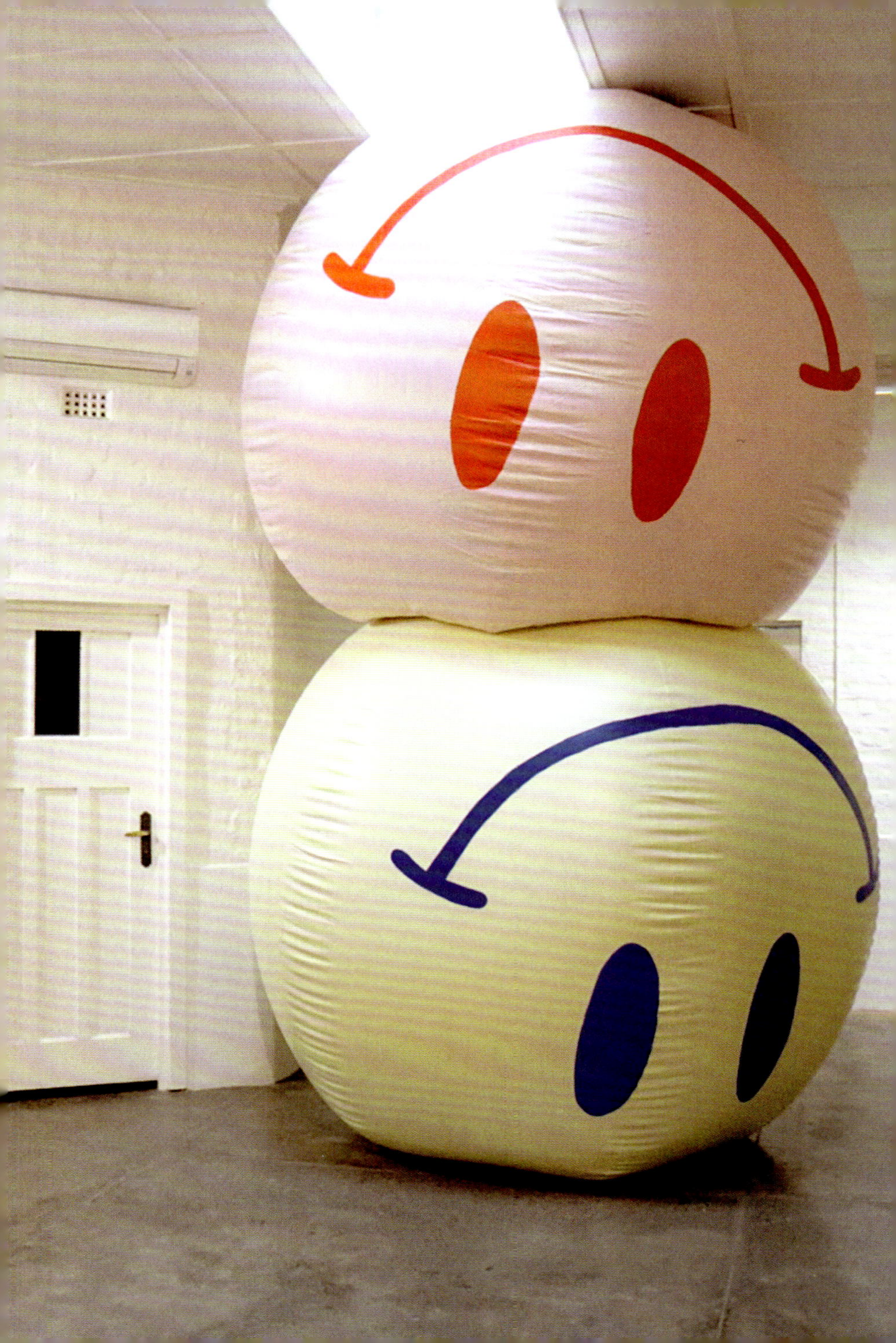

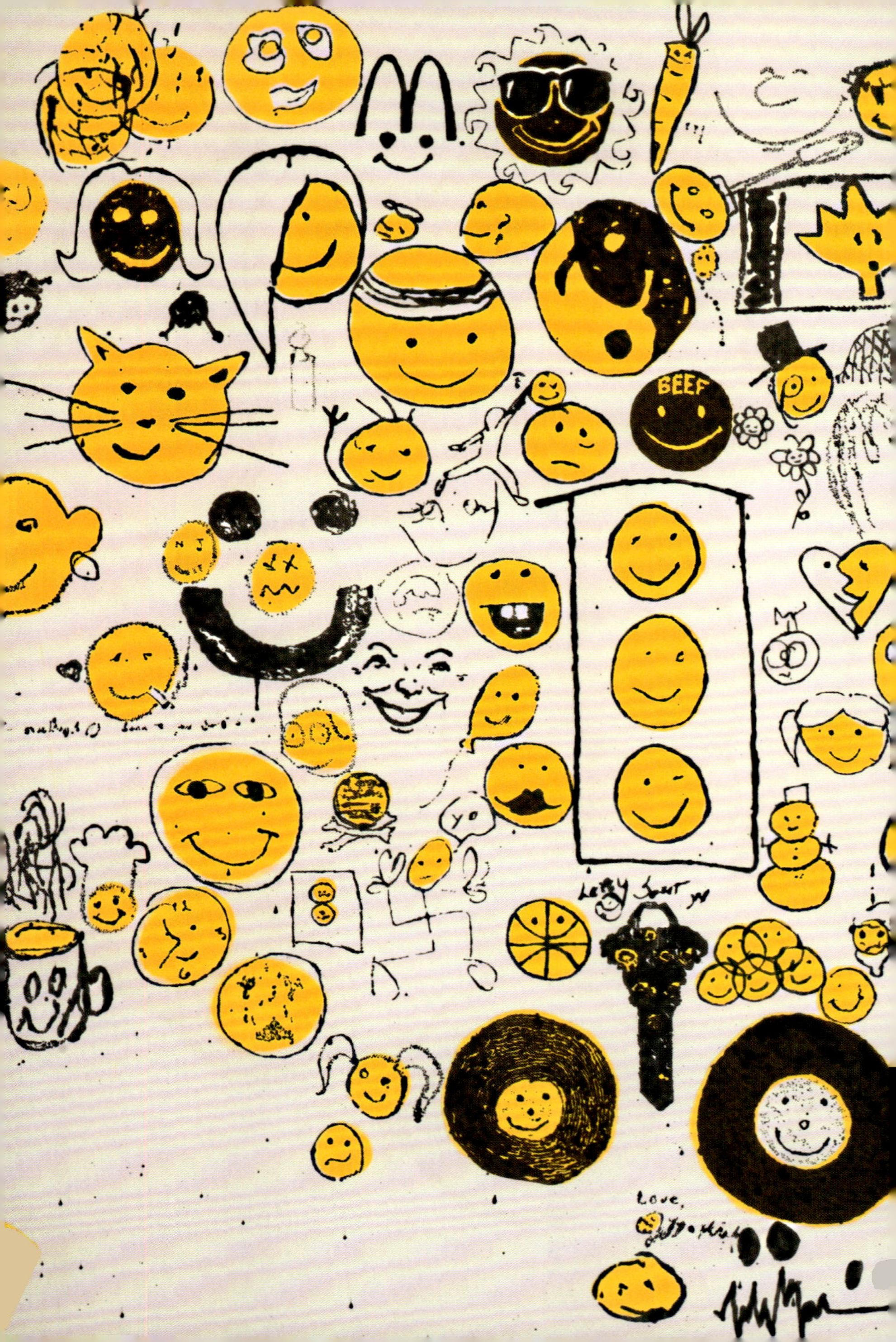

BEEF
love,

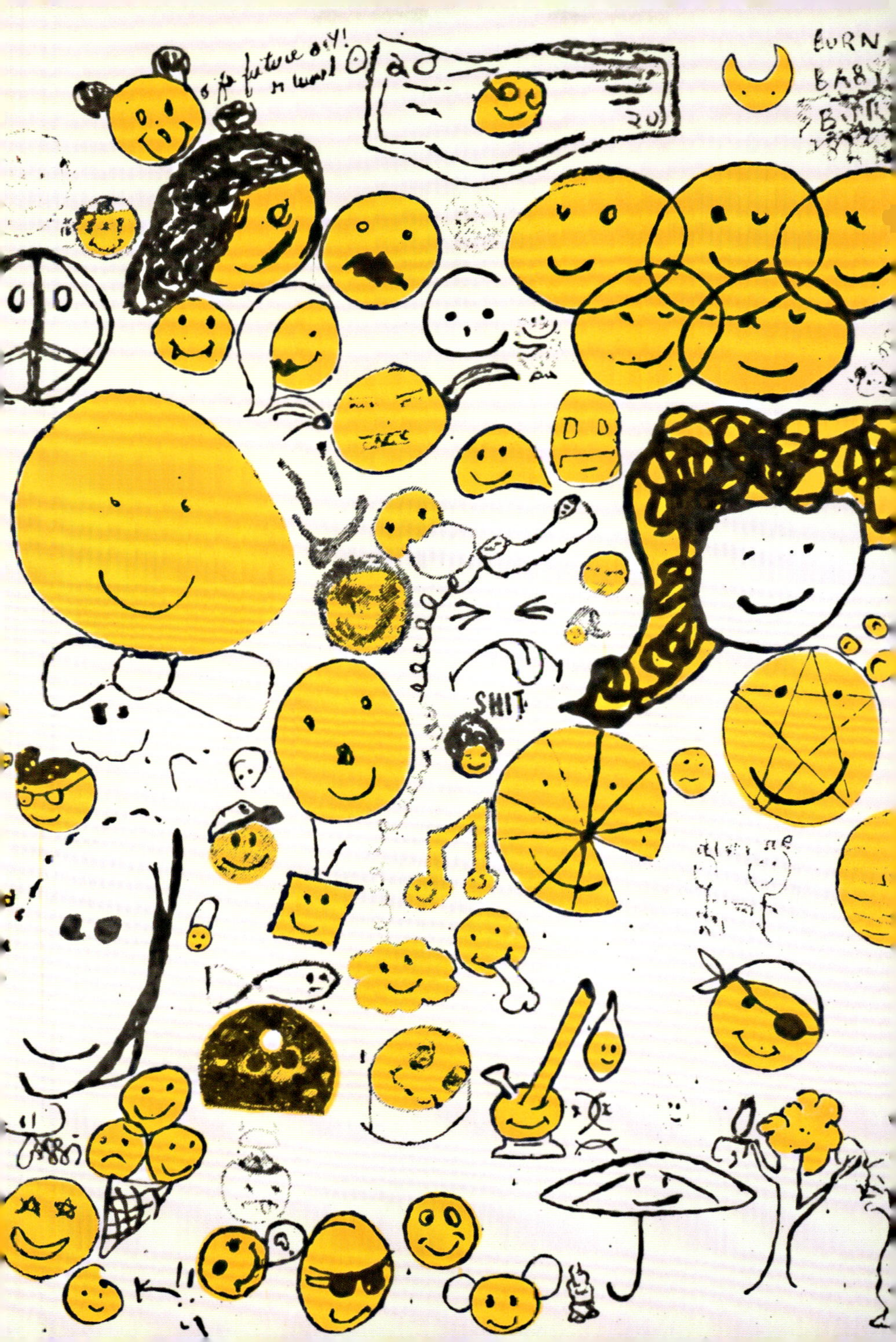
BURN
BABY
BURN
SHIT

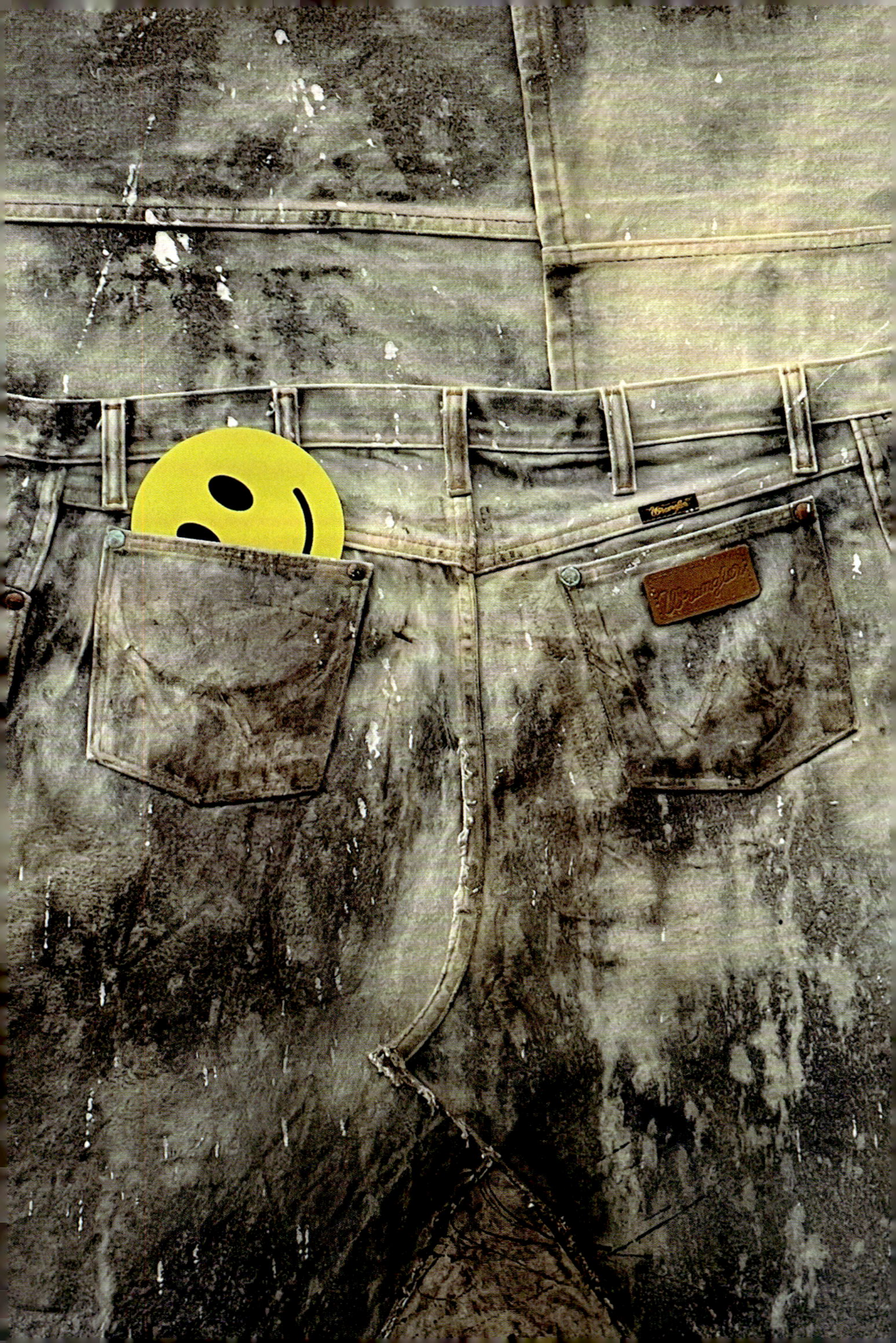

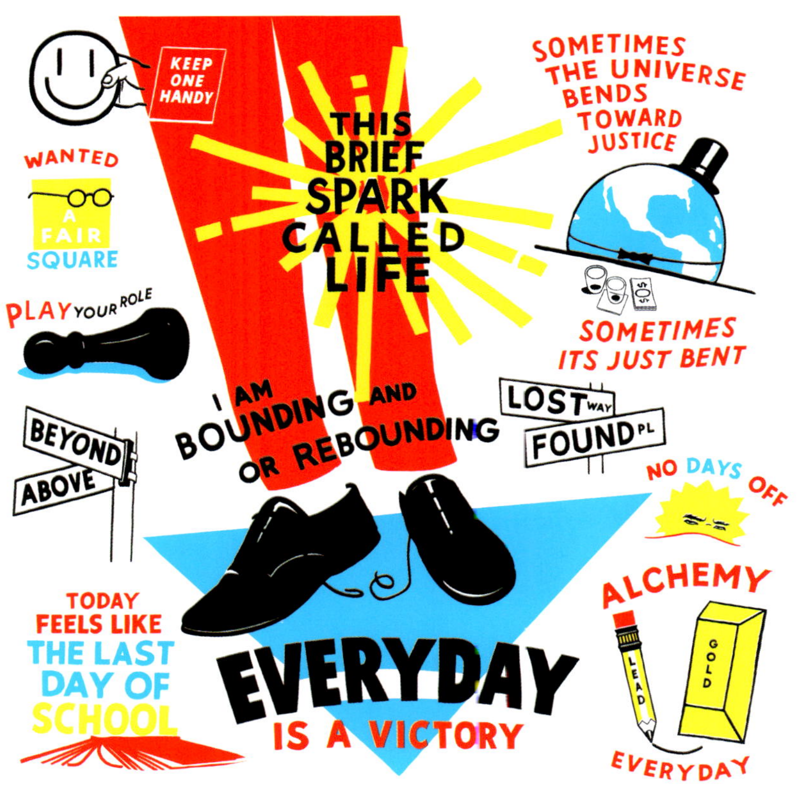
KEEP ONE HANDY
WANTED
A FAIR SQUARE
PLAY YOUR ROLE
BEYOND
ABOVE
THIS BRIEF SPARK CALLED LIFE
I AM BOUNDING AND OR REBOUNDING
TODAY FEELS LIKE THE LAST DAY OF SCHOOL
SOMETIMES THE UNIVERSE BENDS TOWARD JUSTICE
SOMETIMES ITS JUST BENT
LOST WAY
FOUND PL
NO DAYS OFF
EVERYDAY IS A VICTORY
ALCHEMY
LEAD
GOLD
EVERYDAY

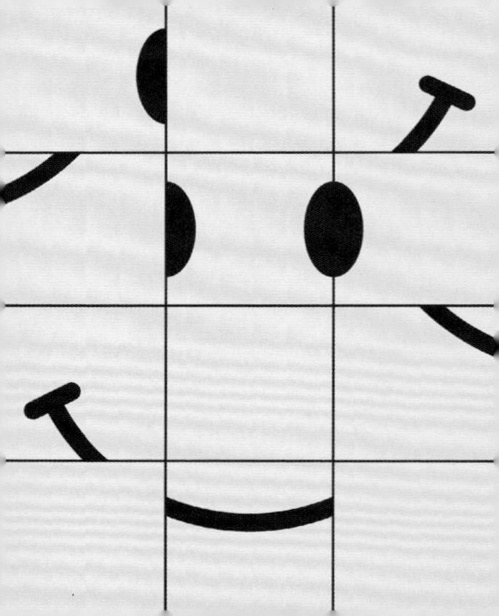

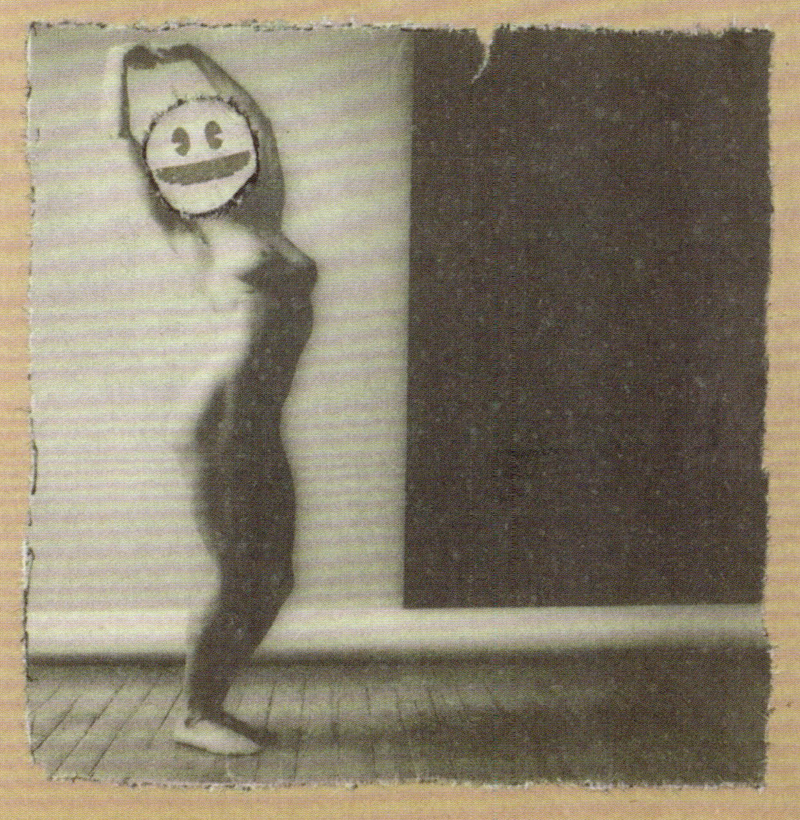

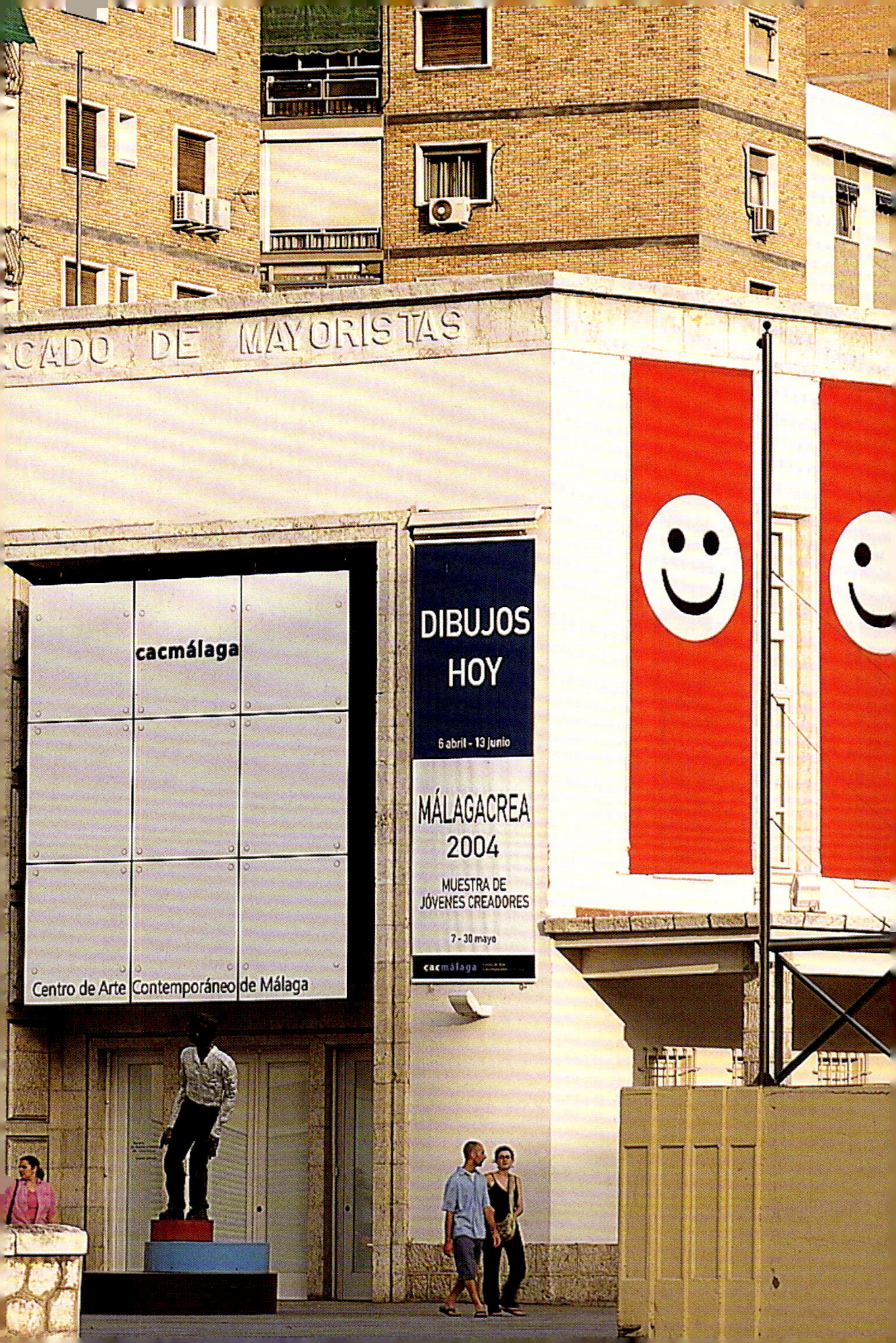
CADO DE MAYORISTAS
cacmálaga
Centro de Arte Contemporáneo de Málaga
DIBUJOS HOY
6 abril - 13 junio
MÁLAGACREA
2004
MUESTRA DE
JÓVENES CREADORES
7 - 30 mayo
cacmálaga

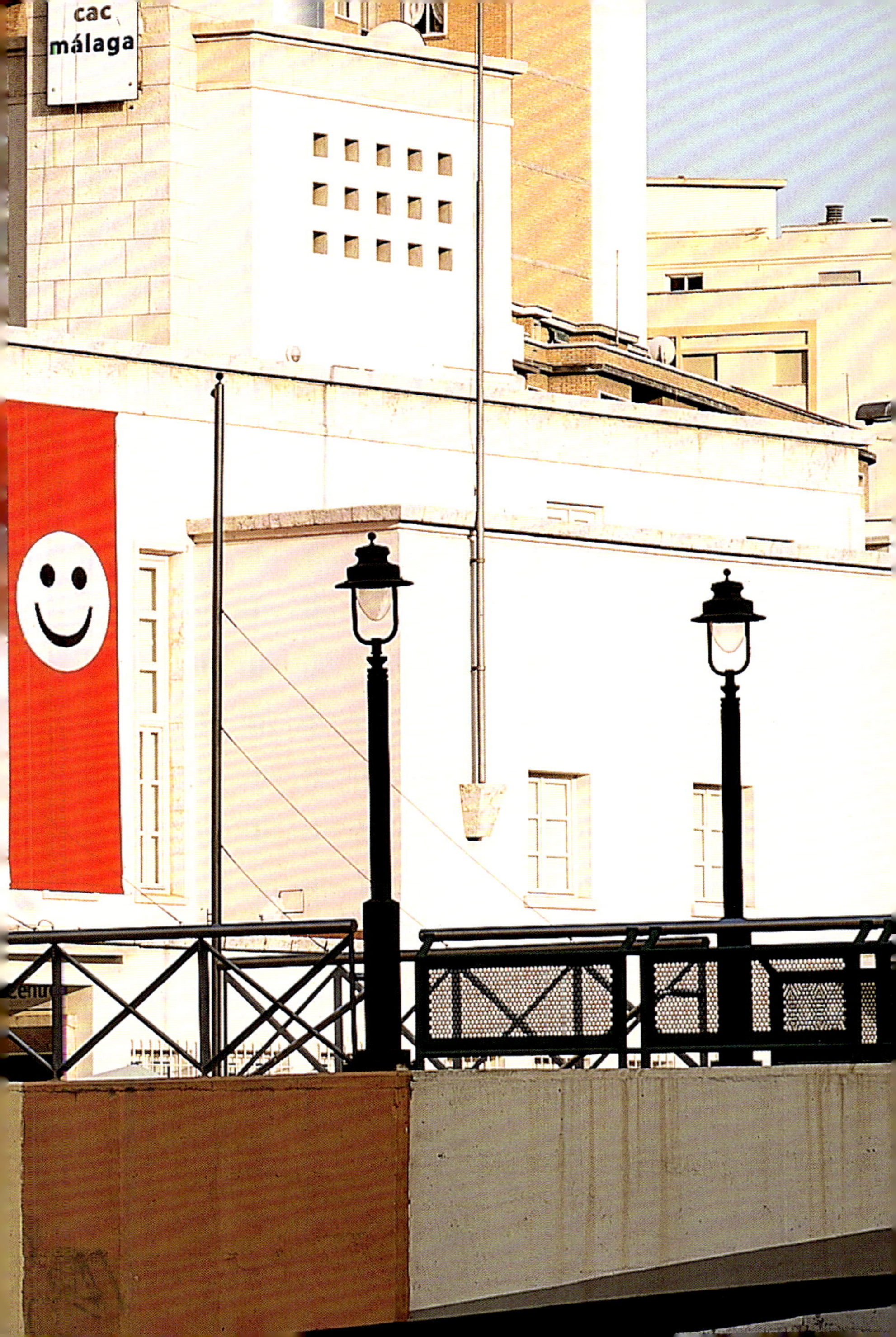

cac
málaga

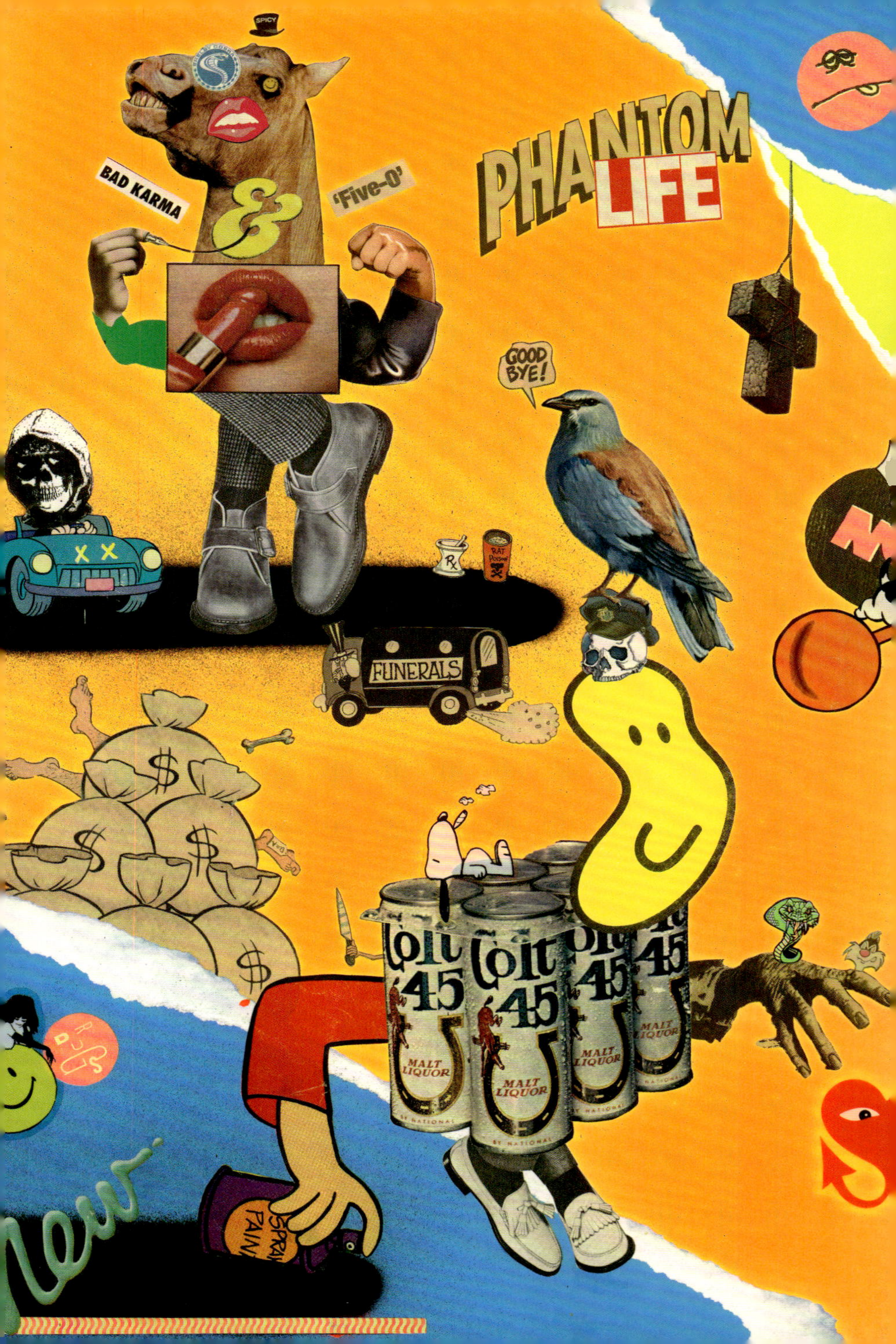

BAD KARMA
'Five-O'
PHANTOM LIFE
SPICY
GOOD BYE!
RAT POISON
Rx
FUNERALS
Colt 45
MALT LIQUOR
BY NATIONAL
SPRAY PAINT

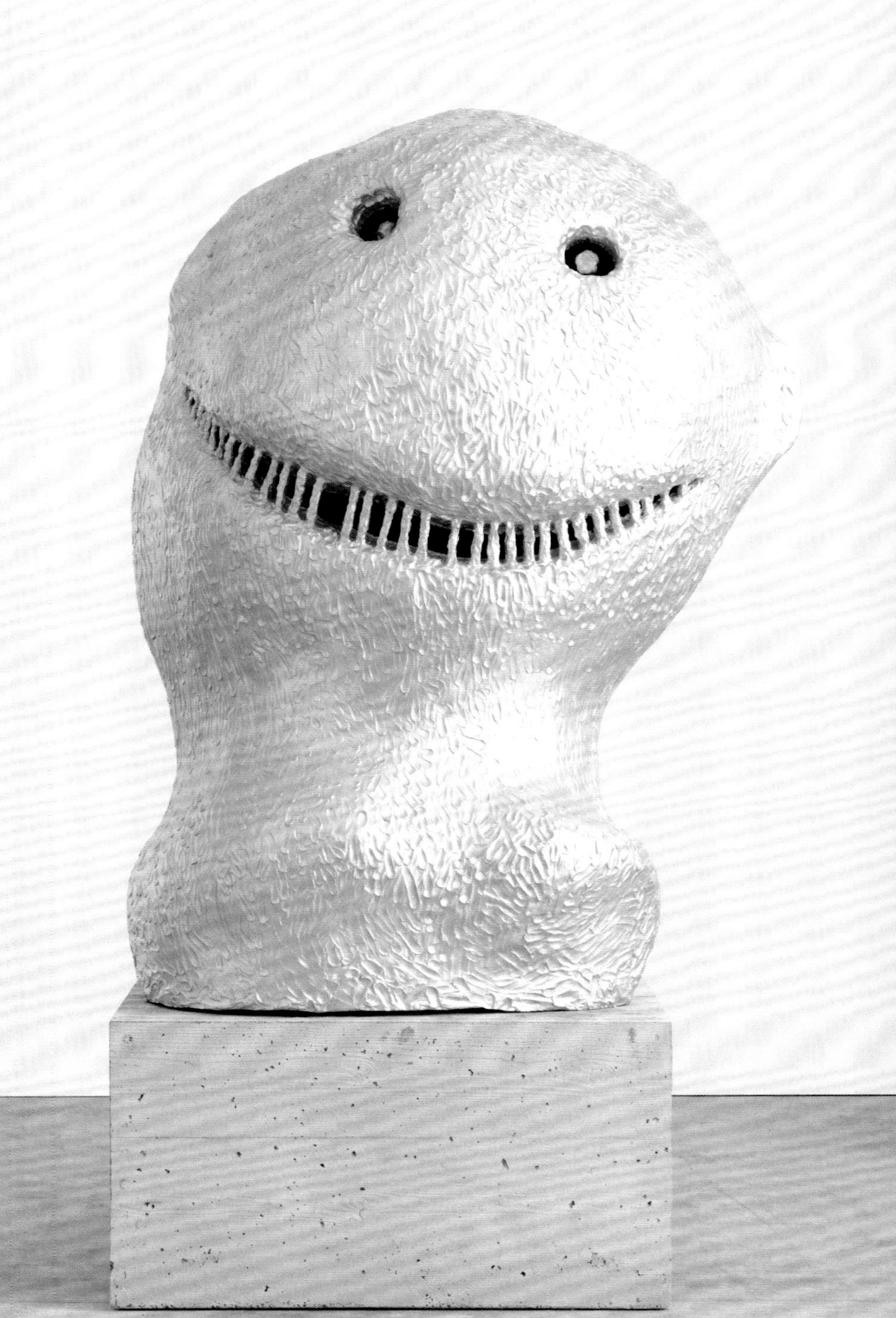

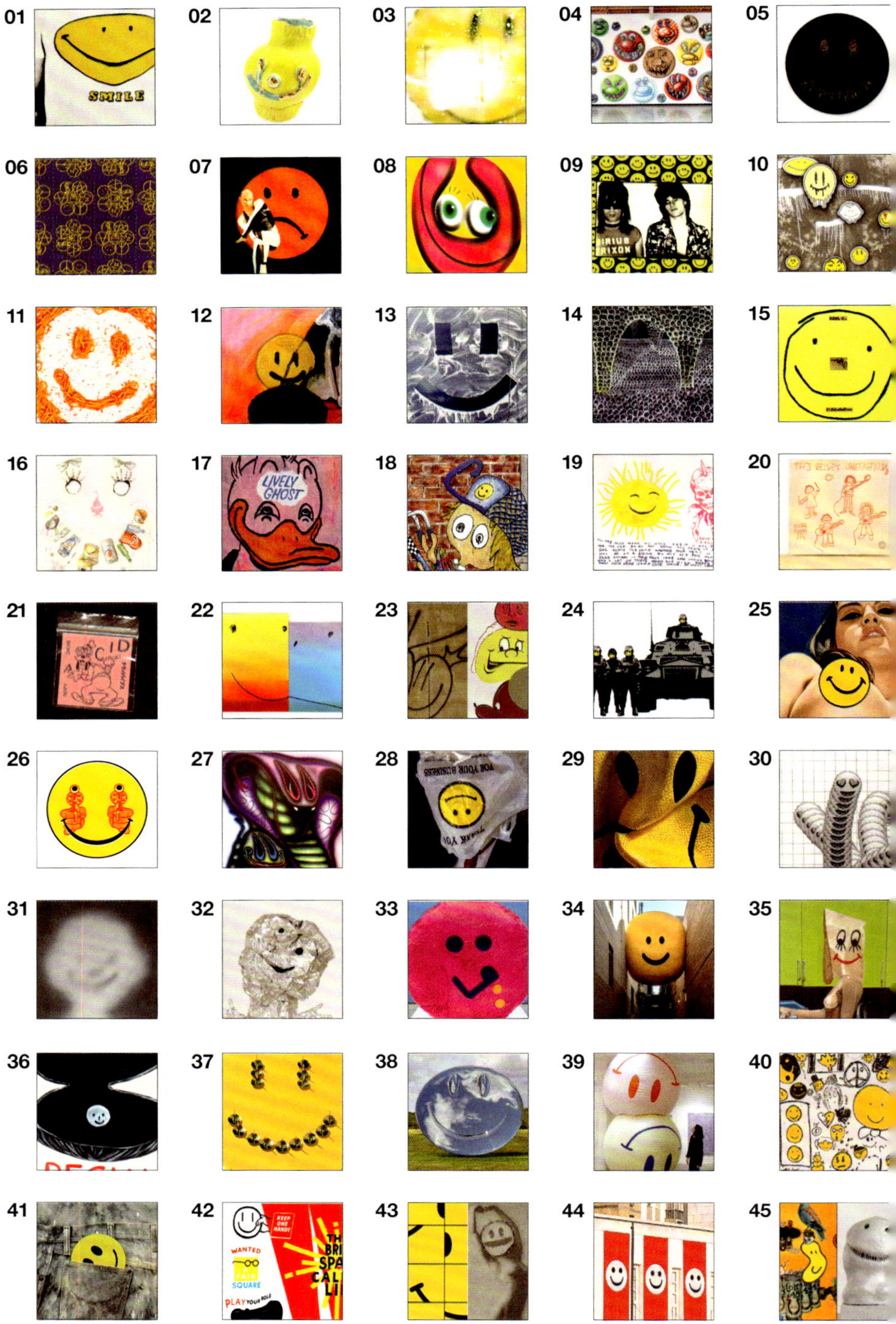

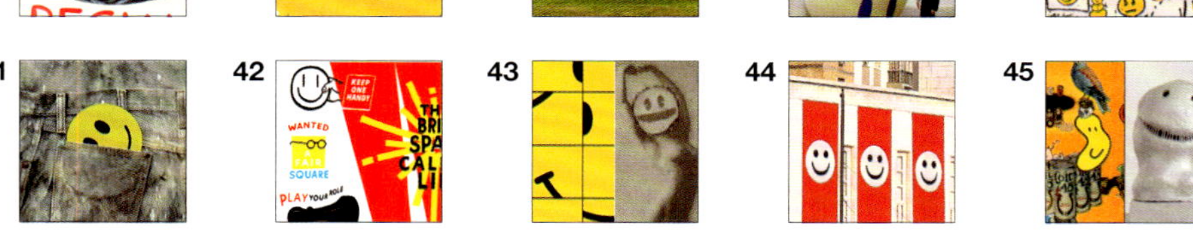

01 Talking Heads "Psycho Killer" 1977 12" single, backcover **02 Dan McCarthy** "Untitled Facepot #151" 2015 Low fire clay and glazes with gold luster 17.5 x 13.25 in. Photo by Kent Pell **03 Marilyn Minter** "Lithium" 2014 Inkjet Print 19 x 13 in. Courtesy of Minter Studio, Salon 94, New York, and Regen Projects, Los Angeles **04 Kenny Scharf** "Moodz" 2020 Jeffrey Deitch, Los Angeles. Photo by Joshua White **05 Ellen Jong** "VELVET TONDO" 2022 One of eight unique phases of the moon, dehydrated ink relief on stretched velvet, on wood panel 46 x 46 x 1.5 in. **06 Fred Tomaselli** "Blotter Logo Mandala Grid" 1991 Yellow print on perforated purple paper 8.75 x 6 in. **07 Michael Clark** "I Am Curious, Orange" 1988 Richard Haughton (dancing man), Courtesy of Michael Clark Company **08 Bráulio Amado** "Killed Smile" for It's Nice That *Printed Pages* SS17 2017 **09 Destroy All Monsters** DAM Magazine 1978 **10 Josh Reames** "Smiling like an idiot" 2020 Acrylic on canvas 68 x 48 in. Courtesy of Josh Reames and Luis De Jesus Los Angeles **11 Maurizio Cattelan & Pierpaolo Ferrari** Courtesy of Toiletpaper magazine **12 Kellesimone Waits** "Halfway Happy Astrokitty" 2022 Acrylic on canvas 11 x 14 in. **13 Justin Metz & Shutterstock** 2019 Digital Art for The New York Times Magazine **14 Joe Roberts** "Wandering The Halls of the Tryptamine Palace" 2015 Acrylic on canvas, 20 x 24 in, Photo by Bill Orcutt **15 Hunter Potter** "Wake Up" 2020 Acrylic, Oil Stick, and Collage on panel 20 x 20 in. **16 Aurel Schmidt** "TGIF" 2019 Colored pencil, graphite, acrylic, watercolor gouache, AriZona Lemonade, Orange Crush, Grape Crush, Diet Pepsi, and burn holes on paper 35.5 x 28 in. **17 John Rogers** "OXY MORON" 2020 Acrylic, paint marker, collage on paper 14 in x 17 in. **18 UFO907** "Show Off" 2019 Aerosol and acrylic on canvas 60 x 65 in. **19 B. Thom Stevenson** "Head" 2019 Acrylic and enamel on cold pressed cotton paper in oak frame with true color glass 47 x 58 cm. Courtesy of V1 Gallery & B. Thom Stevenson **20 Steve Nelson** for The Velvet Underground, Image courtesy Richard Prince **21 Luigi Brusciano (Ignorance1)** "Girls Just Wanna Have Tech" 2018, "Acid" 2018, "Elders Want Techno" 2019 **22 Rob Pruitt** "The Kiss After Brancusi" 2010 Acrylic, enamel paint and flocking on canvas **23A Unknown 23B Barry Mcgee** Untitled 2010 **24 BANKSY** "Have A Nice Day" 2003 Screenprint 13.75 x 38.75 in. **25 Richard Phillips** Untitled (Smiley), 2000 Oil on linen 84 x 62 in. Courtesy of Richard Phillips Studio **26 Ryan Ady Putra** "Untitled" 2020 Digital Art **27 Erik Foss** "Manson Family Picknick" 2021 Water based paint and paint marker on canvas 30 in. x 40 in. **28 Lisa De Boeck and Marilène Coolens** "There's a New Clown in Town" 2020 Courtesy of the artist's and memymom **29 Lucas Price** "Deflationary Asset" 2021 Oil on canvas 90 x 120cm **30 Arno Beck** "Faster than the speed of like" 2019 Pencil and ink drawing on paper 160 x 122 cm. **31 Gerhard Richter Archiv** Dresden State Art Collections, Albertinum Tzschirnerplatz 2, 01067 Dresden, Germany **32 Tom Friedman** "Friend" 2022 Sculpture, oven roaster tins, nuts and bolts 66 x 30 x 16 in. Courtesy of Tom Friedman, Lehmann Maupin, New York, Seoul, and London and Stephen Friedman Gallery, London. Photo by Oriol Tarridas **33 Misaki Kawai** "Moko Moko" (Pink), 2020, Faux fur, felt, wood, steel, 60 x 60 x 12 in. Courtesy of Misaki Kawai and The Hole, NYC **34 Stuart Semple** "I SHOULD BE CRYING BUT I JUST CAN'T LET IT SHOW" for the city of Denver, 2018 Expanded polystyrene foam, acrylic paint and steel 5m x 8m x 3m. **35 Scout Zabinski** "My Sunday Best" 2019 Acrylic on canvas 72 x 48 in. Courtesy of Ross + Kramer Gallery and Scout Zambinski **36 David Shrigley** "You Are Special' 2019 Limited edition screen print on paper 56 x76 cm. **37 Javier Jaén** "How 'Political Correctness' Went From Punch Line to Panic" 2016 The New York Times Magazine, Text by Amanda Hess, Art Direction by Frank Augugliaro **38 Dan David** "Dan-ish Kapoor" 2020 Hand carved Welsh & liquid chrome **39 Elliott Routledge** "Put on a happy face" 2017 **40 Nate Lowman** "Lonely Hearts Club" 2010 Oil and alkyd on canvas 84 x 125 in. **41 Wendy White** "Keep on Truckin" 2018 Repurposed denim and acrylic on canvas, printed cardboard 36 x 36 in. **42 Steve Powers** "This Brief Spark Called Life" 2018 Acrylic on wood panel 24 x 24 in. **43A James Joyce** "Broken Smile" 2020 for New Yorker Magazine **43B Jim Jarmusch** Untitled, 2016 Newsprint collage on paper 7 x 5 in **44 Chapman Brothers** "California Über-Alles" 2004 CAC Málaga **45A Rich Browd** 2012 Collage, risograph, vinyl stickers, spray paint on board 22 x 28 in. **45B Ugo Rondinone** Sunrise. East. September 2005 Cast bronze, silver car paint, concrete plinth, sculpture 200 x 130 x 150 cm. pedestal 58 x 109 x 110.5 cm. Photo by Stefan Altenburger, Courtesy of the artist

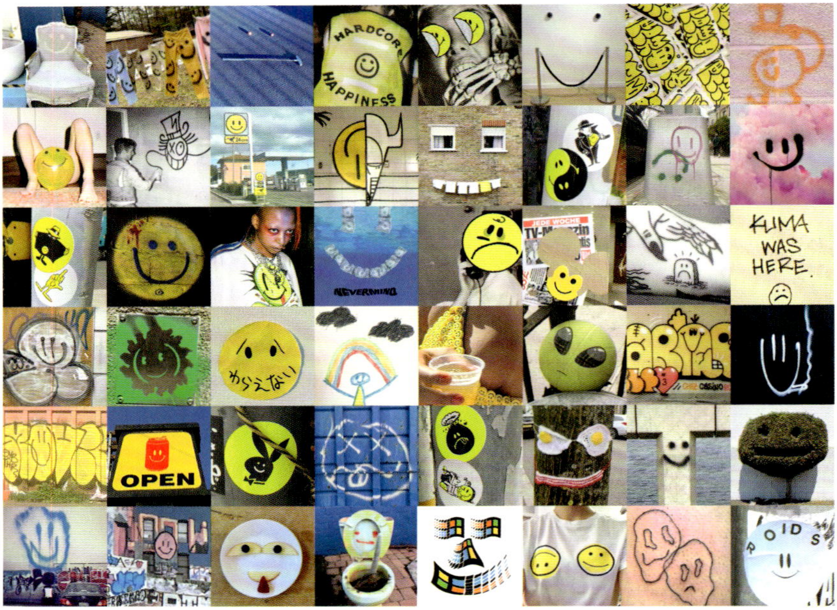

DB Burkeman: A(1), B(7), C(1,2), D(3), E(6), F(2,4) **Rich Browd:** A(3,5), B(6), C(3,5), D(1,2,8), E(1,2,3,4,5,7), F(3) **Amanda Kraemer:** A(2) **Joshua Backus:** A(6) **PEZO D.F.W.:** A(7) **Andrew Jeffrey Wright:** A(8) **Tony Farfalla:** B(1) **Mr.Andre, Photo by Xerxes Cook:** B(2) **Costanza Prandoni:** B(3) **LustSickPuppy:** B(4) **Helga Stentzel:** B(5) **Brooklyn Whelan:** B(8) **Dan Wilson:** C(4) **Ellie Eidelman:** C(6) **Pablo Dalas:** C(7) **KUMA:** C(8) **Max Burkeman:** D(4) **Sarme1:** D(7) **Sergio Guijarro:** E(8) **Snacks in the Grass:** F(1) **Aloha Project:** F(5) **Ariela Kader:** F(6) **Danielle Moalem:** F(7) **Roids MSK:** F(8) **Unknown:** A(4) D(5,6)

All efforts were made to credit photographs. If you see something that is yours please write to info@blurringbooks.com.

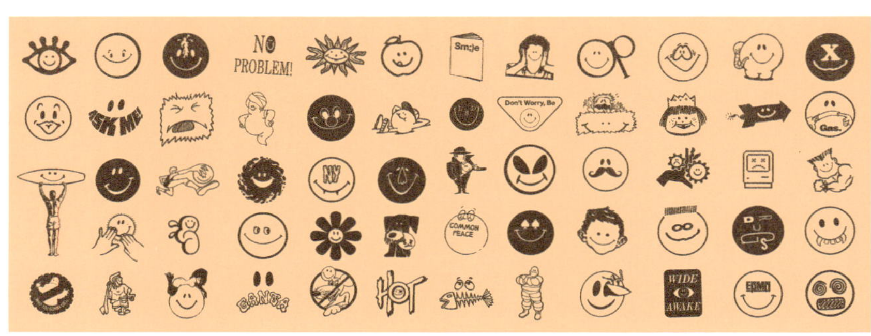

by **Amazing Escapes**

Special Thanks

Anika Jamieson-Cook, Becky Bick, Ben Grandgenett, Camille Beinhorn, Chris Perez, Dave Morgan, David Byrne, Gary Pini, Jacob Daugherty, Jay Wingate, Kevin Lennard, Leo Fitzpatrick, Lisa Marie Conzen, Marianna Peragallo, Matthew Hawton, Matthew Kuborn, Mattias Herold, Michael & Sarah from The Journal Gallery, Nelson Harst, Patrick Shier, Patton Hindle, Pest Control, Stefania Billiato, Sticks & Stones Agency, Theo Elliott, Tony Cox, Valeria Riva

Extra Special Thanks

Aloha Project, Andrew Jeffrey Wright, Anthony Eslick, Ariella Kada, Arno Beck, Aurel Schmidt, B. Denise Gold, B. Thom Stevenson, BANKSY, Baraulio Amado, Barry McGee, Brooklyn Whelan, Chapman Brothers, Costanza Prandoni, Dan David, Dan McCarthy, David Byrne, David Shrigley, Destroy All Monsters, Ellen Jong, Elliott Routledge / Funskull, Erik Foss, Fred Tomaselli, Gerhard Richter, Hunter Potter, James Joyce, Javier Jean, Jim Jarmusch, Joe Roberts, John Rogers / Ghoulorama, Josh Reames, Justin Metz, Ken Kagami, Kenny Scharf, Lisa De Boeck and Marilène Coolens, Lisa Grüb, Lucas Price, Luis Brusciano, LustSickPuppy, Marilyn Minter, Maurizio Cattelan / Pierpaolo Ferrari, Max Burkeman, Michael Clark, Misaki Kawai, Mr. Andre, Nate Lowman, Norman Cook, PEZO D.F.W., Richard Phillips, Richard Prince, Rob Pruitt, Ryan Ady Putra, Scout Zabinski, Stephen Powers, Steve Nelson, Stuart Stemple, Talking Heads, Tony Farfalla / Sticks & Stones Agency, UFO, Ugo Rondinone, Velvet Underground, Wendy White, Zach Britt

---

Curated by
Rich Browd + DB Burkeman

Logistics
DB Burkeman + Sean Johnson

Design
Rich Browd

Production Design
Caroline Maxine Cahill + Christi Catalpa

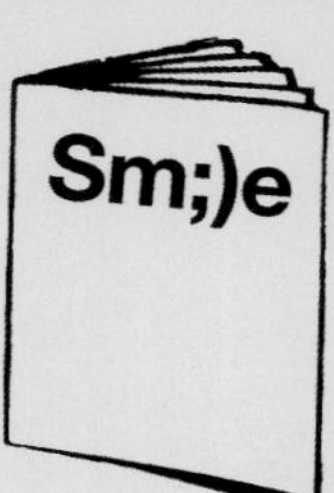
Sm;)e

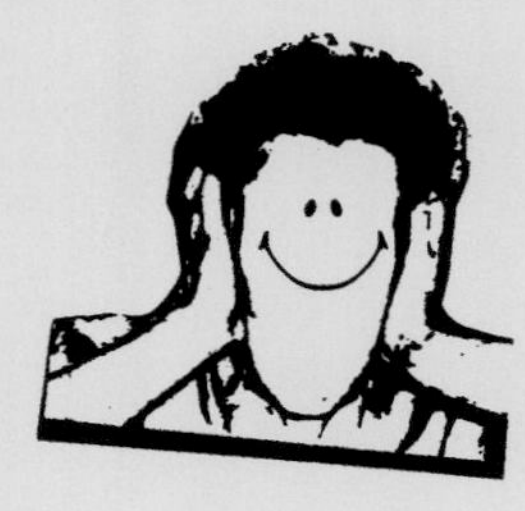

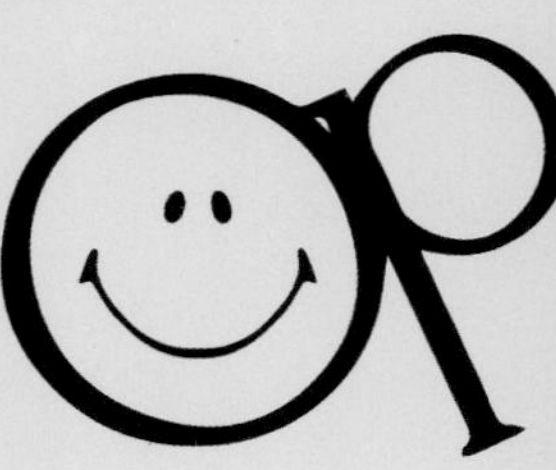

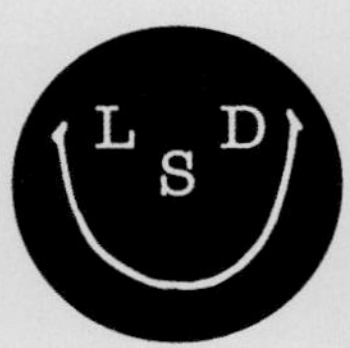
L D
S

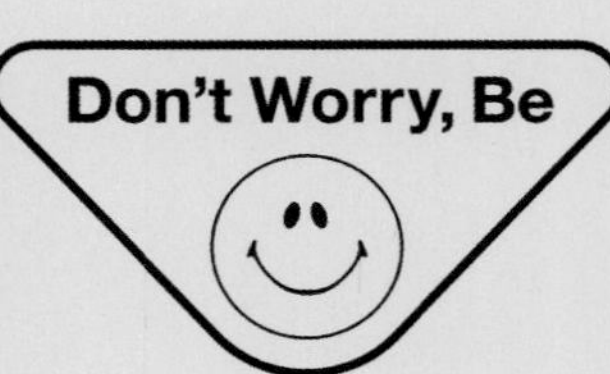
Don't Worry, Be

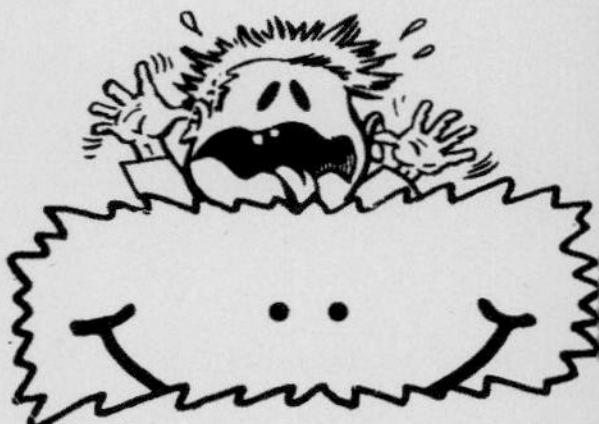

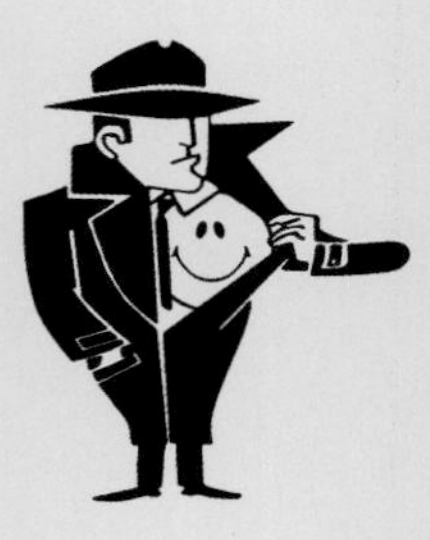

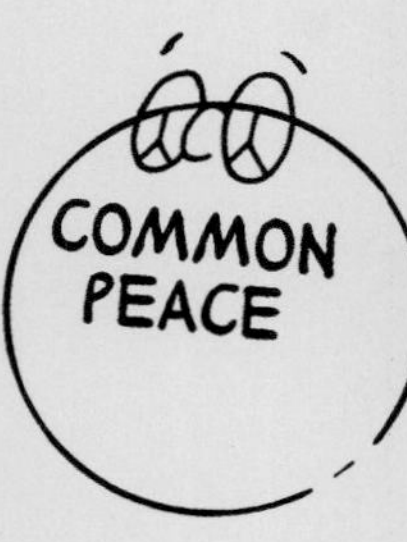
COMMON
PEACE

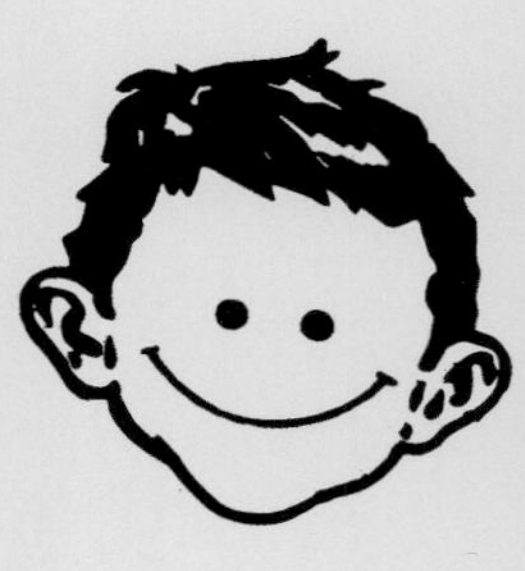

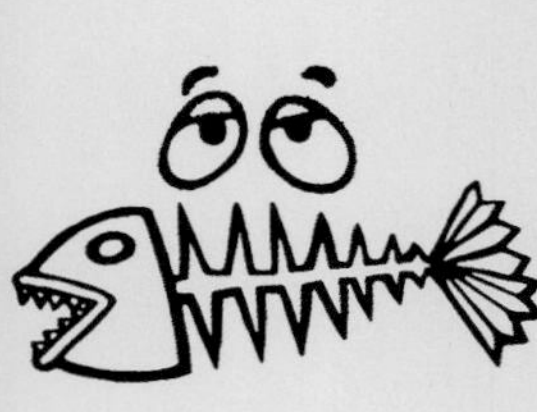

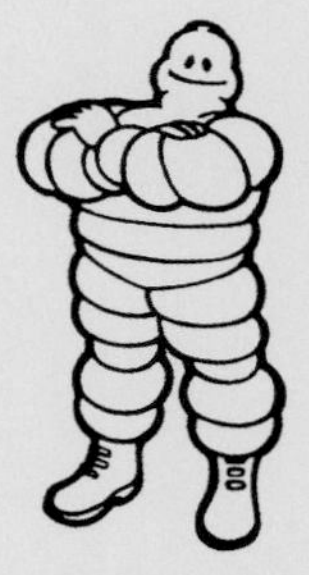

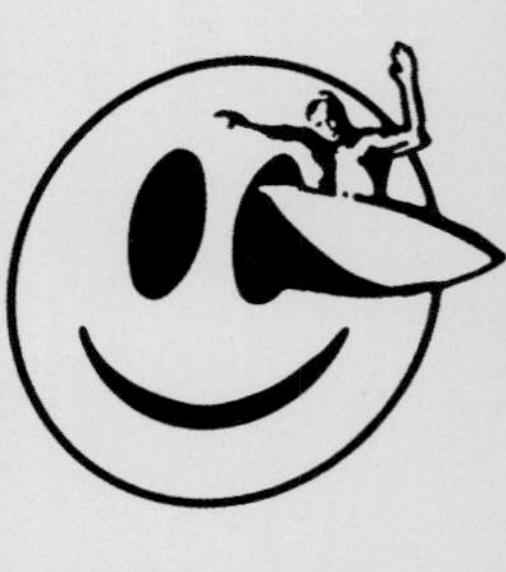